Navy SEAL

Training Guide

Mental Toughness

Lars Draeger

Copyright © 2012 by Lars Draeger.

All rights reserved. No part of this publication may be reproduced, distributed or transmitted in any form or by any means, including photocopying, recording, or other electronic or mechanical methods.

Navy SEAL Training Guide: Mental Toughness/ Lars Draeger

First Printing 2013 United States

ISBN-10: 0-9898229-0-7

ISBN-13: 978-0-9898229-0-9

Contents

Preface vii

The Navy SEALs 1

The Journey – Becoming a Navy SEAL 9

Hell Week 15

Mental Toughness 19

The Four Pillars of Mental Toughness 27

Fear 43

Confidence and Self-Confidence 55

Setting Goals 61

Preparation and Practice 67

Physical Training 73

The SEAL Mindset 79

SEAL Interviews 89

It's Time For Action! 123

Conclusion 127

Preface

The Navy SEAL Training Guide: Mental Toughness was written for people who are striving to improve their current level of mental toughness and self-confidence. It includes information about the U.S. Navy SEALs, and it conveys some of the methods and techniques used by members of this elite unit.

This book can help people from all walks of life to develop these traits, which are often critical to success and high achievement in one's personal and professional lives. Allow this book to serve as the spark that ignites the white-hot flame of mental toughness and self-confidence in your mind, and I honestly believe that it will help you change your life for the better.

Reading this book will cause you to reflect upon the way you have approached difficult or stressful situations in the past. It will enable you to compare your attitudes and actions to those demonstrated by Navy SEALs, men known throughout the world for their mental toughness and their **"I REFUSE TO LOSE!"** mindset.

Congratulations! You've taken the first step toward creating a mindset that will enable you to achieve your dreams, goals, and objectives, whatever they may be!

The Navy SEALs

I think it would be appropriate to provide a brief introduction to the world of special operations to ensure that you have a basic understanding of how the Navy SEALs fit into the overall landscape of America's special-operations community.

Special Operations Forces (SOF) play a significant role in U.S. military operations; the Navy SEALs are part of this group. They belong to the Naval Special Warfare Command (NSWC), which is comprised of:

- approximately 9,000 total members, 2,400 of which are active-duty SEALs
- 700 Special Warfare Boat Operators, known as Special Warfare Combatant-craft Crewmen (SWCC)
- 700 reserve personnel
- 4,100 support personnel
- more than 1,100 civilian employees

The NSWC comprises 10 SEAL Teams, 2 SEAL Delivery Vehicle Teams, and 3 Special Boat Teams. SEAL Teams consist of 6 SEAL platoons each, made up of 2 officers and 16 enlisted personnel. The main operational elements of NSWC include Naval Special Warfare Groups One, Three, and Eleven, stationed in Coronado, California, and Naval Special Warfare Groups Two, Four, and Ten and the Naval Special Warfare Development Group in Little Creek, Virginia. These components deploy SEAL Teams, SEAL Delivery Vehicle Teams, and Special Boat Teams worldwide to conduct training, to participate in exercises and contingency actions, and to carry out combat operations.

SEAL = Sea, Air, and Land

The acronym *SEAL* stands for **Sea**, **Air**, and **Land**, which identifies the environments in which the SEALs are trained to operate. SEALs work in small units, often 2 to 4 men, but sometimes in a platoon composed of up to 16 men. In some situations, such as the operation that resulted in the death of Osama bin Laden, there can be a larger, task-organized unit of several dozen SEALs and support personnel involved.

SEALs are capable of performing specific tasks under various conditions and in diverse environments. When not engaged in actual combat operations, they can be found training around the world, in deserts, jungles, mountainous regions, the Arctic, large cities, and smaller urban areas.

Special Operations

To understand what SEAL teams are trained to do, one must understand the meaning of *special operations*. The following is the definition of *special operations* as defined in military manuals used by U.S. Armed Forces:

> **Special Operations** – Actions conducted by specially organized, trained, and equipped military and paramilitary forces to achieve military, political, economic, or psychological objectives by non-conventional military means in hostile, denied, or politically sensitive areas. They are conducted in peace, conflict, and war, independently or in coordination with operations of conventional forces.
>
> Political-military considerations frequently shape special operations, requiring clandestine, covert, or low-visibility techniques and oversight at the national level. Special operations differ from conventional operations in terms of the degree of physical and political risk, operational techniques, mode of employment, their independence from friendly support, and dependence upon detailed operational intelligence and indigenous assets.

Special operations are different from conventional military operations in that they often require sustained independent actions and operations in situations, circumstances, or environments beyond those that regular military forces are equipped and trained to handle. The selection and training processes combined with specialized skills and capabilities distinguish Navy SEALs and other SOF units from conventional warfare units.

SEAL Missions

SEAL missions require detailed planning and precise execution. SEALs, like other officially designated Special Operations Forces, are trained to perform missions that fall into one of five main categories:

- **Unconventional Warfare** (UW) – Activities conducted to enable a resistance movement or insurgency to coerce, disrupt, or overthrow a government or occupying power by operating through or with an underground, auxiliary, or guerrilla force in a denied area. UW operations include a broad spectrum of military and paramilitary operations, normally of long duration. They are predominantly conducted through, with, or by indigenous or surrogate forces that are organized, trained, equipped, supported, and directed by an external source to varying degrees. These operations include, but are not limited to, guerrilla warfare, subversion, sabotage, intelligence activities, and unconventional assisted recovery.

- **Foreign Internal Defense** (FID) – Activities taken by a foreign government's civilian and military agencies in order to assist another government or designated organization to free and protect its society from subversion, lawlessness, insurgency, terrorism, and other threats to its security. The primary intent is to help the legitimate governing body to address internal threats and the underlying causes of these threats. During recent combat operations in Iraq and Afghanistan the SEALs trained a handful of native citizens. These individuals were trained and equipped with the skills required to conduct various types of military and security-related operations.

- **Direct Action** (DA) – Activities that include short-duration strikes and other small-scale offensive actions conducted as special operations in hostile, denied, or politically sensitive environments, which employ specialized military capabilities to seize, destroy, capture, exploit, recover, or damage designated targets. DA operations may include raids, ambushes, and assault tactics (including close-quarters battle); the emplacement of mines and other munitions; executing standoff attacks by fire from air, ground, or maritime platforms; providing terminal guidance for precision-guided munitions; conducting independent sabotage and anti-ship operations; or recovering or capturing personnel or materials. DA operations are often associated with the pursuit of objectives of great strategic importance, such as the raid that resulted in the death of Osama bin Laden.

- **Counterterrorism** (CT) – Activities taken directly against terrorist networks and indirectly to influence and render global environments inhospitable to terrorist networks. CT operations may be conducted in environments that are denied to conventional forces because of political situations or threatening conditions.

- **Special Reconnaissance** (SR) – Activities that are conducted in the pursuit of information deemed to be of strategic or operational significance. SR operations may be conducted using various overt and covert techniques and tactics.

It is not uncommon for various aspects of two or more of these missions to be executed simultaneously during SEAL operations. Individuals who are tasked with the execution of these missions require high levels of training and skill.

The Trident

The Naval Special Warfare insignia, also known as the "Trident," is one of the most recognizable and most coveted military badges in the world. It was designed and authorized for wear in 1970. The insignia recognizes those service members who have completed the Navy's Basic Underwater Demolition/SEAL (BUDS) training and the subsequent SEAL Qualification Training course.

The Special Warfare insignia was issued initially in silver and gold, following the Navy's tradition of issuing gold badges and insignia for officers and silver ones for enlisted individuals. Today, all SEALs wear the same gold Trident insignia, and it is one of the few Navy skill badges issued in a single color for both officers and enlisted personnel. This change was requested by the SEAL community, as they felt that it would reflect the fact that SEAL officers and enlisted men receive the same training and must pass the same selection process, BUDS, in order to become SEALs.

Trident Symbolism

The Trident consists of four components: an anchor, a trident, an old-style flintlock pistol, and an eagle. Each of the Trident's components has a symbolic meaning.

1. The anchor symbolizes the Navy, the parent service of the SEALs and the premier force for power projection around the world. The old-style anchor is a reminder that the SEALs' roots lie in the valiant accomplishments of the Naval Combat Demolition Units and Underwater Demolition Teams.

2. The trident—the scepter of Neptune, king of the oceans—symbolizes the SEALs' emergence from and unbreakable connection to the sea. The ocean is the most difficult, dangerous, and unforgiving element in which warriors are asked to operate, but it is the environment where the SEALs are most at home.

3. The pistol represents the SEALs' ability to operate in onshore combat operations. If you look closely, you'll notice that the pistol is cocked and ready to fire, a reminder that SEALs maintain a constant level of readiness. They are perpetually prepared to engage our country's foes.

4. The eagle, America's much-loved symbol of freedom, represents the SEALs' capability to be inserted swiftly into battle from the air. Typically, the eagle is placed on

American military badges, emblems, and decorations with its head held high. On the SEAL Trident, the eagle's head is lowered as a symbol of the humility that tempers the awesome strength and military power that's found in every Navy SEAL.

"Of every one hundred men, ten shouldn't even be there, eighty are nothing but targets, nine are real fighters ... We are lucky to have them ... They make the battle. Ah, but the One ... One of them is a Warrior ... and He will bring the others back."

—Heraclitus, 500 BC

The Journey – Becoming a Navy SEAL

In order to appreciate the mental toughness of the Navy SEALs, it's important to have a basic understanding of the long and arduous journey that's necessary to become a member of this elite special-operations unit.

What follows is a general overview of the six stages that Navy-enlisted men and commissioned officers must successfully complete in order to earn the coveted title of U.S. Navy SEAL.

STAGE 1: Naval Special Warfare Prep School
(8 Weeks – Great Lakes, Illinois)

For the majority of prospective SEALs, the journey to becoming a member of the Teams begins after the completion of basic training (boot camp) and assignment to Prep School. This course averages eight weeks in duration, and is supervised by active-duty SEALs and other Naval Special Warfare personnel. In this course, there is a heavy emphasis on physical conditioning. The goal is to condition students to the point where they meet or exceed the established standards for admission to BUDS, and also to ensure their bodies are toughened to the degree necessary to survive the rigors of the subsequent BUDS orientation course and BUDS First Phase.

STAGE 2: BUDS Orientation Course
(3 Weeks – Coronado, California)

During this course students become familiarized with the Naval Special Warfare Training Center at Coronado and get their first real taste of the daily routine associated with being a BUDS student. Physical training (PT) remains a top priority, and the intensity of the PT sessions means they train at a much higher level. The students are taught how to make their way, properly and safely, through the legendary BUDS obstacle course. They also receive basic instruction on some of the equipment that they utilize in First Phase. The students remain in Coronado until they graduate from BUDS or are dropped from the training program.

STAGE 3: BUDS First Phase – Basic Conditioning
(7 Weeks)

The primary mission of First Phase is to eliminate the students who lack the will or the physical ability to successfully complete BUDS. This filtering process is achieved by continuous, rigorous physical-training sessions and other training evolutions. These evolutions are all associated with various training and educational goals, but the reality is that everything about First Phase is designed to push the students to the edge of their perceived physical and mental limitations. As you might expect, First Phase has the highest attrition rate for BUDS classes, historically around 75 percent.

During this phase the standards and scores required to pass various evolutions and graded events are elevated at the beginning of each week, making each week of First Phase tougher than the previous one. In addition to physical training, students are exposed to various water-related training evolutions, both in the Pacific Ocean and in the BUDS training pool. A great deal of emphasis is placed on development of a team mentality and teamwork among the students. The class is broken down into boat teams consisting of six to eight students, and almost every training evolution is conducted as a competition, pitting one boat team against the others, with the students learning very quickly that at BUDS:

"It pays to be a winner!"

The fourth week of this phase is devoted to the infamous and much-feared Hell Week, which is a 5½-day evolution consisting of nonstop physical training and other activities designed to make the students colder and more exhausted than they have ever been. This is, of course, intended to make each student continually reflect upon just how badly he wants to be a Navy SEAL. For many, the rigors of Hell Week are simply more than they can endure, and throughout the week, it is quite common to hear the brass bell being rung three times as yet another student quits the course. Hell Week will be covered in greater detail in the next chapter, since it is such an important factor in the development of the mental toughness that's associated with Navy SEALs.

STAGE 4: BUDS Second Phase – Combat Diving
(7 Weeks)

During this phase students are trained as basic combat swimmers. Successful Second Phase candidates demonstrate a high level of comfort in the water and the ability to perform in stressful, and often uncomfortable, situations. Candidates who are not completely comfortable in the water often struggle to complete this phase.

As you might expect, students spend the majority of their time in the water learning and practicing various surface and underwater skills. Throughout this phase the students will be evaluated regarding their competence and confidence while in the water—both attributes are absolute necessities for a Navy SEAL.

The students are introduced to open- and closed-circuit diving. Both techniques are commonly used in operational units. There is a significant amount of classroom instruction associated with learning both types of diving, making this phase as academically challenging as it is physically challenging. In addition to training to become a combat swimmer, the students are continually challenged by various graded physical-training evolutions, such as timed distance runs, open ocean swims, and, of course, the ever-present obstacle course.

STAGE 5: BUDS Third Phase – Land Warfare Training
(7 Weeks)

During this phase the students get their first real exposure to the many tools and techniques that are related to their chosen profession or specialty. They receive instruction on a variety of small arms, and they spend quite a bit of time becoming proficient in their use. Also covered in great detail is the employment of various types of explosives, land navigation, patrolling, rappelling, marksmanship, and small-unit tactics.

Most of the classroom instruction associated with this phase takes place at the BUDS training compound. The last few weeks of the phase are spent on San Clemente Island, where the Navy maintains live-fire ranges and demolition ranges. Students run through a series of graded evolutions and practical-application exercises during their time on the island.

Throughout this phase the emphasis on physical training remains high and, as always, standards and passing scores for timed runs, swims, and the obstacle course are progressively elevated to ensure that the students find each subsequent week more demanding than the previous one. This continues until the class reaches the long-awaited BUDS graduation ceremony.

STAGE 6: SEAL Qualification Training
(26 Weeks – Various Locations)

Now that the students have successfully completed BUDS, they attend a course known as SEAL Qualification Training (SQT). This training is designed to transition the students from basically-trained combat swimmers and warriors to highly-trained special operators. They must become proficient in many individual and team-based skills, which are essential if they are to operate successfully as a fully qualified SEAL. In essence, this training is very much a "finishing school" that is intended to produce graduates who can be assigned to an operational unit. The goal is to produce SEALs who are immediately capable of performing alongside more seasoned and more experienced teammates.

Students undergo advanced weapons training and extensive instruction in small-unit tactics. They are exposed to advanced demolitions techniques and become more proficient at land navigation during both day and night operations.

Parachute operations—both static line and free fall—are also in the curriculum. The students receive the official designation of "Naval Parachutist" when they complete this phase of SQT.

Various types of communications equipment and extensive medical skills and life-saving techniques that have proven essential during combat operations are covered. This phase also includes cold-weather training in Alaska as well as more extensive training in waterborne operations.

Upon the successful completion of SQT, students are finally awarded the coveted Trident insignia and they are designated as fully qualified Navy SEALs. Each individual will be assigned to an operational unit, where they will undergo more advanced training and, of course, will deploy with their units on various training and contingency operations.

"It is a rough road that leads to the heights of greatness."

—**Seneca, AD 50**

Hell Week

Ask any Navy SEAL to describe the single most powerful, defining moment in his life and he will likely tell you that it was when he realized that he had successfully completed the infamous rite of passage known as Hell Week. This grueling training event consists of 5½ days of continuous running, swimming, paddling a small boat through the frigid Pacific Ocean, and other evolutions designed to push the cold, physically and mentally exhausted students to the very limits of human endurance. During Hell Week, the students are allowed less than a total of 4 hours of sleep throughout the entire week.

The main purpose of Hell Week is to screen out the students who lack the commitment or mental toughness to endure significant amounts of pain, discomfort, exhaustion, and stress. This is necessary because the training that follows Hell Week becomes increasingly challenging, from both physical and academic perspectives. The instructors want to ensure that they have eliminated those who are not truly committed to serving as a SEAL. Typically, 75 percent of the students in a BUDS class fail to make it through training, and Hell Week is the major attrition-producing event.

Throughout the week, be it day or night, the students remain in constant motion as they complete a series of training evolutions built around running, swimming, small boat races, crawling through foul-smelling mud flats, and a number of other events, contests, and situations designed to make the students physically miserable. This, in turn, leads them to wage a constant mental battle with themselves as they contemplate just how badly they want to be a SEAL.

After a couple of days of little to no sleep, combined with extremely high amounts of physical output, many of the students are disoriented and no longer know what day of the week it is. Their voices are hoarse from sounding off for the instructors. Some areas of their bodies have been chafed to the point of bleeding, from being in constant contact with wet sand, which seems to get into every crack and crevice of their bodies.

It is quite common for students to hallucinate during Hell Week, a result of sleep deprivation, and while the students are not really aware of this, the instructor staff remains vigilant to prevent students from seriously injuring themselves. Medical personnel are present throughout Hell Week, and they do their best to patch up students with minor injuries and get them back to their boat teams.

Most of the training evolutions conducted during Hell Week are competitive in nature, pitting one boat team against another. As is the case throughout BUDS, the instructors reward the winners of these competitions. It is common for them to grant a winning boat team permission to lie down for 15 minutes of sleep or to allow them to stand close to a warm fire, while the losing boats teams are punished unmercifully.

During Hell Week the instructors mercilessly harass, ridicule, and taunt the students, often using bullhorns to broadcast their nonstop barrage of insults, sarcastic comments, and offers of "hot coffee and donuts" for those who have had enough and want to quit BUDS. This, of course, is the main goal of the instructors—to get the mentally weak to cave in and ring the bell three times.

BUDS students often mistakenly believe that Hell Week is all about physical strength and endurance, but those who manage to survive it and continue on to become SEALs say that mental toughness is the critical factor required to get through this evolution. Once they pass Hell Week, the vast majority of students will indeed go on to become fully qualified SEALs.

"First say to yourself what you would be, and then do what you have to do."

—**Epictetus, AD 100**

Mental Toughness

All Special Operations Forces in the U.S. Military undergo rigorous selection and training programs that are designed to push men past their perceived physical and mental limitations. Since World War II, when the famed Underwater Demolition Teams were formed, the Navy Special Warfare community has earned a reputation for operating what many believe is the most demanding selection course in our Armed Forces.

The SEAL community, via the infamous BUDS training course, seeks to separate the strong from the weak in order to ensure that only the most committed men become members of this special brotherhood. They do this by putting BUDS students in a constant state of mental turmoil, which causes a nearly constant battle inside their minds, forcing those aspiring to become SEALs to face the "quit, don't quit" decision dozens of times per training day.

Aside from identifying those capable of serving as SEALs, the training is also designed to produce a warrior that is supremely confident in his abilities and those of his teammates. Ask any SEAL and he'll tell you that, while there are many qualities required of a frogman, there is one that stands out as the single most critical factor in determining whether or not a man can make the cut and survive BUDS: mental toughness.

Extraordinary mental toughness forms the foundation upon which a SEAL is trained. This mental toughness enables him to achieve success when the odds are stacked against him. It is the trait that causes him to demonstrate a refuse-to-lose mindset, and it is the underpinning of the SEAL ethos and the unswerving loyalty and dedication that he has toward his teammates.

Equally important to the success of the Seal Teams is the fact that every SEAL forever holds himself and his teammates accountable to this high standard. The reality is that one day—as has happened so many times in the history of the Teams—the lives of many may depend on the actions of a few, or perhaps even a single teammate.

The Definition of Mental Toughness

The topic of mental toughness has been debated for decades, and to the best of my knowledge there is still not a standard, widely accepted definition for the term. It is used by military trainers, coaches of all types, business leaders, and sports psychologists. From an athletic perspective, the term is used to describe an athlete that possesses the ability to stay focused while under very stressful circumstances and to perform well. Military leaders use it to describe the traits necessary to enable a warrior to remain calm in extremely dangerous situations, including ones that pose a danger to that person's life, and to make the appropriate decisions or perform the tasks required to accomplish the mission.

The famous sports psychologist Dr. Jim Loehr of the Human Performance Institute defined mental toughness as follows:

> "Mental toughness is the ability to consistently perform towards the upper range of your talent and skill regardless of competitive circumstances. It is all about improving your mind so that it's always on your side; not sometimes helping you nor working against you as we all know it's quite capable of doing."

Think for a moment of a person who is known for being mentally tough. Odds are that this person has established a reputation for achieving consistently superior results under a wide range of conditions or in various types of situations involving stress, pressure, and risk. He or she likely maintains a positive attitude and approach to achieving his or her goals and remains focused on winning despite numerous distractions and changing circumstances. Also exhibited is the ability to remain resilient and motivated when dealing with setbacks, disappointing results, and mistakes and being able to remain focused on the desired end state: successful accomplishment of stated goals or objectives.

While I have known many mentally tough SEALs and operators from other SOF units, I must say that some of the most mentally tough people I have ever met were not in the military. Meeting and knowing some of these people caused me to understand that mental toughness was not a quality exclusive to SEALs, other SOF operators, or even world-class athletes. I learned, through observation and interaction with these people, that some of the most physically frail individuals are often as mentally tough as any SEAL is—maybe even more so.

I've seen people battle cancer for years, enduring countless sessions of chemotherapy, knowing all the time that their chances of survival were low, yet they kept fighting. I had a friend who was struck by throat cancer in his early 40s. He suffered through two long years of chemo and radiation treatments, to no avail. Throughout his battle with cancer, he exhibited a level of determination and a fire in the gut that was impressive and humbling at the same time. I don't think he ever stopped believing that he would ultimately beat the disease, and he remained upbeat and positive right up until the very moment he left this life. He was never in the military, but I can tell you without reservation that he had the type of mental toughness that SEALs need and that you likely want to develop.

The point I am trying to convey is that, while all SEALs are mentally tough, one does not have to be a Navy SEAL to become mentally tough.

Can Mental Toughness Be Taught?

I believe that mental toughness can be taught, and the results of various research and studies validate my belief. While it is apparent that some individuals have higher levels of mental toughness as a result of their childhood experiences—sports, economic and social factors, parental guidance, etc.—it does appear that this quality can be cultivated and developed through specific training and education.

Because of the real-world demands placed on special-operations forces such as the SEALs, it is critical that members of such units be pushed to their physical limitations in order to replicate the stress levels associated with combat situations. This type of physical rigor is also useful for athletes and others engaged in activities that include a high level of physical exertion or effort. But there are also many professions, activities, and environments in which physical exertion and the necessity for physical strength and fitness are limited or even nonexistent, yet still require a great amount of mental toughness in order to perform at optimal levels.

Physicians, trial attorneys, stock traders, airline pilots, business owners, and entrepreneurs are some examples of professions in which the need for physical prowess is typically limited, yet a person's success can often be directly impacted by the presence or absence of mental toughness. Additionally, people involved in various "personal battles"— such as situations at work; dealing with family or personal relationship problems; coping with health issues, drug addiction, alcoholism, obesity—need a great amount of mental toughness in order to push past their limitations, deal with the challenges facing them, and follow whatever steps are necessary to achieve their goals.

SEALs Talk about Mental Toughness

I thought it would be beneficial to include some quotes and comments made by Navy SEALs on the topic of mental toughness. While each of them has his own personality and way of expressing his thoughts on the topic, I think you'll agree that their comments all reflect the **"Fire in the gut"** and **"It pays to be a winner"** mentality that is instilled in SEALs from their first day at BUDS.

"Mental toughness is doing whatever is necessary to accomplish the mission."

"You simply cannot be a Navy SEAL without being mentally tough. You wouldn't make it through BUDS, and you certainly wouldn't be able to operate in combat if you weren't. SEALs must have the mental ability to block out physical pain and fear, while remaining highly focused on whatever is required to achieve victory."

"In my opinion, mental toughness is the ability to remain calm when others are overcome by fear or panic, and being able to do whatever needs to be done to win."

"Mental toughness is not letting anyone or anything break you."

"Mental toughness is not being affected by anything that might degrade your ability to achieve the mission you've been assigned. It is the ability to perform well under the worst conditions possible."

"No matter what happens, I simply refuse to lose. To me, it's really that simple. I approach anything thought to be difficult with an attitude of 'I'll do this or die trying.'"

"It means that whenever most people would make excuses why something can't be done, I focus on finding a way to get it done."

"Mental toughness is the belief that, as long as I'm breathing and my brain is functioning, I have the ability to succeed at any given task."

"I think mental toughness is a man's ability to defeat the voice in his mind that is telling him to quit."

"I've seen a lot of mentally tough guys during my time in the Teams, and the common trait they possess is that they all believe that adversity brings out the best in them and that there's always a way to win."

"The ability to stay focused when ordinary men would buckle under the pressure or be consumed by fear."

"Being mentally tough means that you can have your arm shot off and, if necessary, pick it up with your other hand and use it as a club to kill the enemy."

"My platoon did a hit on a house in Iraq, and I came face-to-face with an insurgent. For a brief moment, we looked into each other's eyes. I walked out of that house and he didn't."

"I was never able to shake my fear of heights and never enjoyed jumping out of an airplane at twenty thousand feet, yet I did so hundreds of times over my twenty-year career. I simply decided that my desire to serve in the Teams was stronger than the fear I felt toward jumping. SEALs aren't immune from fear; they simply refuse to let it affect them in a negative way. That's what mental toughness means to me."

In summary, mental toughness is a quality that plays a critical role in achieving success in all aspects of life, personal and professional. It is directly associated with physical toughness in many environments, such as with the Navy SEALs and other military units, but is also a key ingredient to success in professions and situations in which little or no physical activity takes place. What is important is that mental toughness can, in fact, be studied and practiced; and individuals from all walks of life can develop this quality to the point where it makes a positive impact on their lives and the attainment of success, however defined.

"We will either find a way or make one."

—Hannibal, 218 BC

The Four Pillars of Mental Toughness

The attrition rate for BUDS classes has historically averaged around 75 percent, which means about 8 out of every 10 students in any given class will fail to complete the course successfully. While most SEALs view this attrition rate as an indicator that the selection process has remained as demanding as it has always been, senior SEAL leaders have always tried to identify methods and techniques that would enable them to better identify candidates that would be more likely to successfully complete BUDS. Even though the Navy wants only the very best men to be able to qualify to serve as a SEAL, there is still a great amount of expense associated with recruiting and training prospective SEALs only to have the vast majority of them fail to complete the course.

In an attempt to avoid this significant waste of time and money, the Navy has conducted numerous studies over the past few decades, all aimed at refining the SEAL recruiting process and reducing overall BUDS attrition. While most of the studies did produce actionable data that enabled SEAL recruiters and mentors to better prepare recruits for the physical rigors of BUDS, classes consisting almost entirely of these more physically prepared students still produced attrition rates - the historical levels of approximately 75 percent.

SEAL leaders realized that, despite the fact that incoming BUDS students were the most physically prepared and capable in the history of the course, they were still failing at a very high rate. Thus, it became obvious that the attrition problem—and the high costs that are associated with this—could not be remedied with better physical preparation alone. Rather, something had to be done to help BUDS students to develop the mental toughness required to successfully endure the rigors of the course.

Research Results

Psychologists assigned to the Naval Special Warfare Command continued to study BUDS students. They were able to identify four techniques that most of the graduates were instinctively using to help them remain motivated and resilient through the rigorous training. As these four techniques were studied in more detail, psychologists found that the techniques were quite similar to those used by Olympic and professional level athletes, and by other high-achieving individuals in various professions associated with great amounts of stress, risk, and danger. These techniques are collectively referred to as the Four Pillar Technique of developing and maintaining mental toughness, motivation, and resolve in situations associated with fear or threat stress.

Over time, the refinement of these mental techniques by Navy psychologists resulted in an organized program of instruction that has been integrated into the BUDS curriculum in an attempt to teach the students how to unleash the mental toughness that many already have within them. BUDS classes that were exposed to the Four Pillar Technique produced graduation rates that were approximately 32 percent better than classes without the training. As added proof that these mental techniques are effective, a high percentage of SEALs continue to use them while serving in operational units and even after they leave the Navy and enter various professions and occupations.

The Four Pillar Technique

The following information will provide an introduction to the individual elements of the Four Pillar Technique and how they are used by students at BUDS and by SEALs assigned to operational units.

Pillar 1: Goal Setting

When Navy Special Warfare psychologists conducted studies to identify why so many BUDS candidates failed to make it through training, they found that almost all candidates that successfully completed the course and went on to serve as SEALs had used a technique in which they established short-term, mid-term, and long-term goals for themselves throughout the course.

For instance, rather than thinking about another several months of grueling BUDS training, a successful student instead would focus on what he was actually doing at that moment and turn it into an "event" that had to be successfully completed. So during a 6:00 a.m. physical-training session on the grinder (grinder PT sessions are quite difficult both physically and psychologically), rather than focusing on getting through the entire 90-minute session, the student would simply focus on getting through one set of calisthenics at a time. If the PT instructor directed the class to do a set of 50 pushups, the student would isolate his focus on this task and think about nothing else until it was completed. He'd do the same for the following set of flutter kicks, blocking out all other thoughts and distractions until that set was done. He'd do the same for the next set of jumping jacks, and so on for each of the many dozens of sets of calisthenics and exercises typically done during a grinder PT session.

By focusing on one set of exercises at a time, BUDS students are able to focus completely on the immediate task at hand and avoid thinking negative thoughts like: *We just started and I'm already really tired. There's no way I'll be able to make it through another hour of this and then be able to pass the four-mile timed run later in the morning.* Many BUDS graduates readily admit that at various times during the course they were so physically and mentally exhausted that the only way they could maintain focus and stay motivated was to convince themselves to *Hang on until lunch* or *Keep running for another minute* or *Just make it through this run of the obstacle course.*

One of the SEALs interviewed for this book stated that during BUDS he would literally break down each training day into dozens of separate events starting from the moment he woke up. Once he was done shaving and brushing his teeth, he'd say to himself, "OK, got that done—you're a winner! Now, let's get dressed."

Next he would focus on getting dressed in the proper uniform for the day's first training event, and when he did that he again would reaffirm mentally that he had once again "been a winner" and was ready for the next "event," which was to clean his barracks room with his roommates.

After successfully completing this task (and "winning" once again), he'd fall out for morning formation with the rest of his class and run a mile to the chow hall for breakfast. He viewed this run as yet another of the several dozen short-term micro-goals to be tackled during the course of the next 8 to 10 hours.

Using this technique enabled him to avoid focusing on the rather dreadful fact that he had so much ahead of him, months of exceptionally difficult training, before his class was scheduled to graduate from BUDS. Instead, he reduced a grueling and psychologically intimidating six-month course into thousands of micro-goals, and the successful completion of them ultimately led to him standing with the rest of the survivors of his BUDS class on graduation day.

Psychologists often refer to this micro-goal technique as "segmentation," and studies have shown that it can be effective for people pursuing almost any type of goal. Personal goals, such as losing weight, getting healthier, getting better at a sport or hobby, or gaining admission to a prestigious university, can be achieved using this technique, as can professional goals, such as being hired by a specific company, getting selected for a promotion, or gaining some form of recognition or achievement within one's profession. This is a time-tested technique that you should consider utilizing in all aspects of your life.

Pillar 2: Mental Imagery

Another technique that was found to be common among those who successfully completed BUDS was a student's ability to utilize mental imagery of him successfully completing a specific task or challenge.

For example, during Phase Two of BUDS one of the training evolutions requires students wearing scuba gear to perform various emergency procedures and corrective actions to resolve problems with their equipment, all of which must be executed while the student remains underwater. During this evolution the instructors will attack the students and snatch the regulators from their mouths, close scuba-tank air valves, disconnect hoses from the tanks, tie the hoses in knots, and other such things. Most of the students are still very new to being underwater and wearing scuba gear, and they are not yet completely comfortable and confident in this environment. Adding to the mental stress of this evolution is the fact that if a student panics and surfaces without permission he fails the event. If he performs the proper corrective actions too fast or too slow, he will also be deemed a failure. If the instructors feel he didn't appear confident and relaxed while executing the corrective actions, they will also fail the student. If he fails to pass the evolution after a few attempts, he will be dropped from training and rolled back to another BUDS class, which is a most unpleasant thought for any BUDS student.

Navy psychologists found that a majority of the successful students had experienced a significant degree of anxiety and apprehension for this training evolution. They knew that it was considered one of the most difficult graded events within the entire six-month course and the reason for a high number of students washing out of BUDS completely. To say that this training evolution induces a high level of anxiety and fear of failure among BUDS students is an understatement, and if you ever get the chance to speak with a SEAL, ask him about it and I'm quite sure he'll concur with my comments.

The psychologists discovered that almost all of the students that successfully completed this evolution on the first attempt had utilized a technique in which they visualized themselves going through the various emergency actions they'd been taught and would be tested on. They knew exactly what to do to remedy all situations and problems the instructors could possibly impose upon them; and they repeatedly went through these actions in their mind in the days and hours prior to the actual test. They mentally rehearsed being attacked from the rear by two or more instructors who would snatch the masks from their faces and regulators from their mouths or would remove the scuba tanks from their bodies. As a result of this visualization, once the evolution was actually underway, the students were able to ignore the fact that they were being attacked and focused entirely on calmly solving the problems being presented to them.

The use of mental imagery is also used by BUDs students prior to other training evolutions, such as timed runs of the

BUDS obstacle course, exceptionally difficult timed open-ocean swims, and distance runs, as well as during many of the demolition- and weapons-related testing. BUDS students are tested, formally and informally, many times per day, and the fear of failure and of being dropped from training is constant. Not only do they have to deal with their own mental battles and avoid succumbing to negativity, thus quitting the course, but they have to live with the perpetual fear of not meeting standards for various events and tests. Adding to the stress is that fact that, in some instances, the criteria for passing an evolution are not shared with the students. In instances such as this, the instructors will simply say something like, "The standard is one hundred percent effort. When the whistle blows to start this run, give it everything you've got!"

All of this is designed to identify those capable of keeping their composure and ability to focus on specific tasks and actions while under duress. In other words, a SEAL must be able to remain focused and do whatever's necessary during the most stressful, dynamic combat situations. The only way to ensure they can do so is to screen them for these traits during BUDS.

Mental-imagery, visualization, and mental-rehearsal techniques are used by people in many professions, such as police, firefighters, paramedics, teachers, public speakers, and, of course, countless athletes at the world-class and professional levels. I have spoken with surgeons who say they mentally rehearse the steps they will take during a multi-hour knee-replacement surgery or a quadruple-bypass operation. Likewise, numerous high-level athletes have told me that they visualize themselves properly executing various techniques and moves or "scoring points" prior to an event.

I think it is obvious that this technique works for Navy SEALs as well as for people in many other walks of life. If you're not using it as you pursue your goals, no matter what they may be, I strongly encourage you to consider doing so. As the BUDS instructors continually say to the students, "It pays to be a winner!" I am sure you'll agree that most of the winners you know and associate with think of themselves as such. I think there's a high probability that they have utilized the mental-imagery technique to help them get to where they are today.

Pillar 3: Self-Talk

Psychologists have long known how important positive and constructive self-talk can be for any individual. They know how much of a positive impact it can have on a person as they undergo periods of great stress or anxiety, or when they are engaged in the pursuit of a significant and highly desired personal or professional goal, objective, prize, achievement, or form of recognition.

Research studies have shown that the average person thinks at a rate of 1,000 to 5,000 words per minute. Even when a person is alone, sitting silently, there is an active "conversation" taking place within his or her mind. Common sense would tell us that the more positive and upbeat these conversations are, the more beneficial they would be toward a person's outlook, attitude, and feelings regarding any aspect of their life. In other words, we are in complete control of the conversations that are taking place within our minds, and we should ensure that they are of a positive nature. I assure you that if you ever get an opportunity to speak with a Navy SEAL, he will agree that his ability to engage in positive self-talk was one of the primary factors in his successful completion of BUDS.

I think it is fairly obvious to anyone with even a casual knowledge of BUDS that the students undergoing this grueling training course are constantly faced with graded evolutions of ever-increasing difficulty. This results in a student having to 'talk to himself' hundreds of times per day and remind himself that all of the pain he's enduring is the price to pay to achieve his goal of becoming a Navy SEAL and that nothing, no amount of pain, will cause him to fail to achieve his goal.

Numerous studies of successful BUDS students show that there is a very high correlation of successfully completing the course and becoming a SEAL and an individual student's ability to engage in continuous, positive self-talk throughout the course. So important is this technique—not only to BUDS students but to SEALs in operational units engaged in combat operations—that it has been embraced by the SEAL community as one of the four pillars of mental toughness and self-confidence expected of and demonstrated by all Navy SEALs.

A very experienced career SEAL, discussing positive self-talk, shared that, when he was going through BUDS, he would constantly remind himself that he'd trained well prior to the course and that many men had already completed the course, and there was no reason why he could not do so. "I kept telling myself that I was physically stronger and a better runner and swimmer than many men who made it through

BUDS, and that the only reason why they were SEALs was because they refused to quit," said this now-retired Senior Chief Petty Officer. He further stated, "I realized after a few weeks that I was actually a faster distance runner than a few of the BUDS instructors. I was also much bigger than several of them, and probably physically stronger than they were. These observations reassured me that the Teams weren't looking for Olympic-level athletes; they were looking for minds with Olympic-level mental toughness, whether it was in a one-hundred-fifty-pound body or a two-hundred-fifty-pound one!" He went on to say that throughout BUDS he'd repeat a "mantra" in his mind that said things like "I'm a winner. I'll never quit!" and "I'm going to finish this run!" or when enduring an evolution in the frigid Pacific Ocean, "If this is as cold as it gets, I can do this!"

Another SEAL related that he also engaged in positive self-talk throughout BUDS, telling himself things such as "I ran great yesterday, and I'm going to kick ass on the O-Course today!" and "I'm going to pass this test. I'm ready, and I'm going to be a winner once again." During one brutal motivational session that required him and his mates to perform various lifts with a 300-pound log known as "Old Misery" he heard his fellow boat team members straining under its weight while being taunted by the instructors. He said that he kept thinking to himself, *It's not as heavy as I thought it would be* and *Just keep moving, don't stop* and *I'm tougher than Old Misery.*

Of the four pillars of Navy SEAL mental toughness, I think that self-talk is the one that you are probably most familiar with and, perhaps, already practicing to some degree. I believe that it is possible for anyone to use this technique and for those already using it to become more effective at it, which would promote higher levels of mental toughness and self-confidence.

Pillar 4: Arousal Control

When a person is exposed to stressful situations that elicit fear, anxiety, anger, nervousness, worry, and other negative emotional reactions, the human brain will typically trigger the release of cortisol, adrenaline, and other chemicals into the bloodstream. These chemicals, especially cortisol and adrenaline, usually cause an immediate response by the body, such as elevated heartbeat, increased rate of breathing, tension in the major muscle groups, shaky hands, and other signs that the body has recognized some kind of threatening situation and is instinctively preparing to defend itself either through fight or flight.

This arousal response is a perfectly normal and predictable reaction by the human body, but it is also a potentially negative one that can greatly diminish a person's critical thinking, decision making, and fine motor skills. For obvious reasons, Navy SEALs who engage in combat operations—many of which are quite complex and often associated with tremendous pressure to succeed, such as the bin Laden raid—cannot afford to allow themselves to be controlled or otherwise to have their effectiveness reduced by their body's normal response to this type of arousal, and over time the SEAL community has discovered ways to counter negative arousal response and render it insignificant during the execution of SEAL operations.

One of the most common arousal-control techniques taught to and used by SEALs is a breathing technique that some refer to as "4 x 4 breathing." Simply stated, the 4 x 4 breathing technique is executed by inhaling deeply, as though you are trying to fill up your lungs, for four seconds, and then exhaling in a steady and even manner for four seconds. This sequence must be continuously repeated for at least one minute to be effective, and many SEALs find that doing it for longer periods of two to four minutes produces even better results.

Medical doctors say that the 4 x 4 breathing technique is an effective way to trick the human brain into replicating certain calming and stress-reduction aspects associated with deep REM sleep patterns, which are the periods of sleep that provide the most benefit from a rest and recuperation perspective. I have utilized this technique countless times and know firsthand that it really works.

BUDS students use this technique on a daily basis as they prepare for training evolutions such as timed distance runs and open-ocean swims, while waiting to begin a run of the obstacle course, or prior to jumping into the pool for a "drown-proofing" session. Many SEALs continue to use this arousal-control technique long after they graduate from BUDS.

I think all SEALs will agree that being overcome with emotions, such as anger, fear, or anxiety, is not conducive for operating at high levels of critical thinking, decision making, and combat effectiveness. For these warriors, failing to adequately control arousal can lead to diminished performance at a time when the stakes are high to them personally, to their teammates, and, at times, to the national interests and prestige of the United States of America.

In Summary

As stated earlier in this chapter, BUDS classes that were taught the Four Pillar Technique and how to apply it to their training increased their graduation rates by 32 percent. Clearly this training had a profound impact on many students, many of whom obviously had the "right stuff" to complete BUDS but simply needed some education and guidance to bring out that which already resided within them so they could perform at a high level of intensity and commitment on a sustained basis throughout BUDS and during their subsequent careers as SEALs.

Obviously, many people—myself included—believe that this kind of mental-toughness training can be utilized by individuals in various professions or by those who are pursuing goals that are associated with a high degree of difficulty. I can see how these techniques could benefit athletes at every level, students who aspire to gain admission to medical or law programs at elite colleges and universities, people who aspire to leadership positions in industry, people who struggle with issues and situations requiring self-confidence, and people who have had difficulty in the past with personal issues, such as their relationships with other people, attempts at losing weight, or other health-related issues.

In summary, I think that the training used by Navy SEALs to develop mental toughness can benefit people of all ages and from all walks of life. I've personally witnessed, in many situations, how a person can greatly elevate their performance and probability of being successful by increasing their mental toughness.

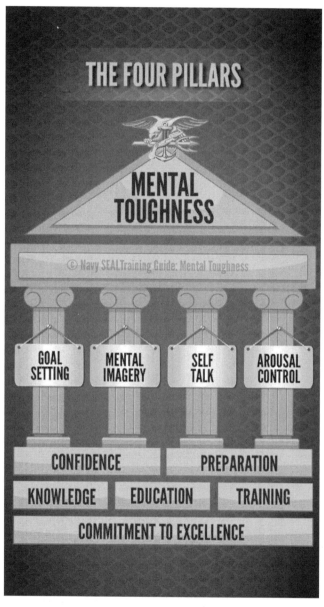

"You have power over your mind—not outside events. Realize this, and you will find strength."

—Marcus Aurelius, AD 161

Fear

It is an understatement to say that technology has greatly changed how war is conducted over the past several centuries. That said, it is also true that today's warriors react to the stresses of combat, especially that which brings about fear, in the same way that our club-, spear-, and sword-wielding ancestors did. No amount of technology has been able to change the fact that men engaged in combat operations or other high-risk activities have to face the fear of injury and death. Simply stated, fear can cause SEALs to fail in combat. Knowing this, the Naval Special Warfare community has spent a great amount of time and effort studying the topic, and in this chapter I will share some of the knowledge gained from this research.

To operate effectively in combat situations, SEALs must be able to remain focused on the use of highly technical equipment, make rapid decisions, and execute physical tasks that require both fine and gross motor skills, often while being shot at by a determined enemy. Success depends on a mind that is conditioned to expect fear and knows how to neutralize its impact on human performance in the most stressful conditions imaginable. When asked about the topic of fear, a veteran SEAL officer told me that, in his opinion, there were two kinds of SEALs: those who admit they've felt fear and those who are lying. He went on to state that "SEALs are human, and all humans are vulnerable to feeling fear. Our training is what enables us to control fear to a degree most humans cannot."

Before I get any further into this chapter, I want to explain that I have attempted to write in a manner that non-military readers would be able to understand. In other words, I have tried to explain things in "plain English" so that people who have no previous exposure to the military, combat operations, and the Navy SEALs can understand the lessons and information that I am trying to convey. That said, this particular chapter may seem to be a bit more academic, more like a college textbook, than other chapters in the book. I feel this is a necessity given that this chapter refers to various scientific studies and mentions specific parts of the human anatomy.

The Physiology of Fear

To learn how to control fear, you must understand your body's natural response to it. Fear stimulates the sympathetic nervous system, which is responsible for the fight-or-flight response that is programmed into our brains as a result of millions of years of human evolution. This response has been present since the first cavemen fought with one another over food and faced off against an animal that was trying to kill them. The famed Prussian General Carl Von Clausewitz described the human response to fear in this way: "The fog of war can prevent the enemy from being seen, a gun firing when it should, a report from reaching a commander." This response can cause men in combat to lose the ability to perform the simplest of tasks, such as reloading their weapon, and to become physically weak, to the point they cannot remain standing or cannot muster the strength to operate equipment or perform tasks that they've performed successfully hundreds, or even thousands, of times in the past.

The stimulation of the sympathetic nervous system while a human is under stress is called "threat stress," and fear can elicit threat stress. This in turn will trigger a hormonal response that will degrade the performance and level of execution of a combat soldier if he is not trained to control this response. In plain English, when faced with a dangerous or threatening situation, real or perceived, the human body prepares itself to cope and survive by entering a state of high physiological arousal through the release of various hormones, including adrenaline and cortisol. The major physiological responses to fear and threat stress are:

- **Increased heart rate and breathing.** This is the body's way of enabling a more rapid rate of oxygen exchange to certain areas, such as large muscle groups and major organs.

- **Queasiness or "butterflies."** Because blood flow is being diverted away from the digestive system and toward major muscle groups and organs, the abdominal area is being deprived of oxygen, which produces a queasy or fluttering sensation.

- **Dizziness.** Increased rate of breathing can often cause a level of hyperventilation, which can flood the brain with too much oxygen, causing dizziness.

- **Dry mouth.** There are several physiological reasons for this, but the main one is that increased rate of breathing has a drying effect on the mouth and throat area.

- **Sweating.** The increased heart rate, breathing and sudden surge of blood flow to large muscle groups generates heat, which the body attempts to regulate through sweating.

- **Tremors and shakes.** Since blood flow is diverted from smaller muscles associated with fine motor skills to large muscles and major organs, they are deprived of oxygen and become more difficult to control.

- **Dilated pupils.** Blood flow is increased to the eyes, causing the pupils to dilate, better enabling the person to see potential threats.

- **Slurred speech.** Blood flow is diverted away from areas of the brain associated with secondary functions such as speech, and this often causes a person to slur his words and speak at a slower-than-normal rate.

The Importance of Heart Rate

Of all of the physiological responses to fear listed above, experts believe that increased heart rate has the most negative impact upon performance. In his highly acclaimed book *On Combat*, retired U.S. Army Lieutenant Colonel David Grossman describes how heart rate affects performance under stressful conditions. His research, which has been validated by previous and subsequent studies, indicates that, in general, the higher the heart rate, the more a human body relies on instincts when responding to dangerous situations, threats, and problems. The issue with this is that during times of great stress a person's instincts are often wrong. In a combat situation, an incorrect decision or poorly executed physical action can result in death, injury, or mission failure.

To further illustrate his findings, Grossman defines five conditions based on a person's heart rate and assigns a color to each of them:

- **White.** The normal heart rate range is 60 to 80, and this is classified white. At this heart rate thought processes are normal, fine motor skills are intact, and gross motor skills can perform daily activities.

- **Yellow.** When fear causes the release of adrenaline, the heart rate begins to climb. When it reaches the next level, the heart rate is 80 to 115, and this is condition yellow. Condition yellow is different from condition white because the level of vigilance increases. Condition yellow could be compared to walking down a dark alley known for violence.

- **Red.** Condition red is when the heart rate is between 115 and 145, and this is considered to be the optimal performance level. Condition red has the benefit of increased strength, and improved reaction time and speed, but the person will have a loss in fine motor skills.

- **Grey.** The next condition is grey, a heart rate from 145 to 175. This condition is reserved for members of special-operations units and athletes who train to work at this level. The only difference between red and gray is that the person has trained and enabled his body to work in this condition for a prolonged period of time.

- **Black.** The last condition is when the heart rate is above 175, and this condition is labeled as black. In condition black, irrational behavior occurs, such as inability to move, loss of bowel control, loss of urine control, and gross motor skills are at the maximum level. Escaping from the threat is typically the only thing that the person wants to do.

It is important that you realize that in the majority of situations elevated heart rates are less the result of physical stress than that of psychological stress. Think of a time in your life when you were sitting down or were not moving at all, yet your heart was racing as though you'd just done several wind sprints. This is exactly what is being discussed here—the ability of the mind to cause physiological responses in one's body and, of course, the need to control these responses so they do not have a negative impact on performance.

The five conditions of heart rate established by Colonel Grossman are not to be considered "etched in stone" and not to serve as literal boundaries that cannot be crossed. It is a fact that many highly trained people engaged in a variety of activities often operate at peak efficiency, with heart rates as high as 200 beats per minute (bpm) for hours at a time. World-class cross-country skiers and Formula 1 race-car drivers are two examples.

One scientific study of seasoned Army Special Forces operators indicated that the soldiers with the best results on various tests and tasks could do so at heart rates at or just below 175 bpm for prolonged periods of time. Operators that experienced heart rates above 175 bpm turned in some of the worst results in the study. But the general thought amongst military leaders and medical personnel is that a warrior can be educated and made aware of how his mind, when experiencing fear or threat stress, can affect his body, and be trained on how to minimize stress's negative impact on performance.

How to Control Fear

The first step in controlling fear is to recognize the physiological effects it produces, especially those associated with elevated heart rates. The ability to recognize these physical effects and to neutralize them is the key to maintaining a calm and steady state of mind during periods of great stress, which, of course, enables a person to operate at adequate levels.

Untrained individuals often believe that raw courage is all that is necessary to defeat fear and its effects, and many SEALs were once included in this group. SEALs now know that it is critical that they understand the physical and emotional causes of fear, and to be able to identify situations in which the body will begin reacting to it. If one is able to anticipate situations that will initiate the body's coping mechanism for fear (the physiological responses listed above), the proper steps can be taken to thwart these bodily reactions and maintain lower heart rates. Thus you will be able to perform fine motor skills, such as being highly accurate with weapons during the close-quarter battle situations SEALs often encounter. Although impossible to eradicate completely, fear can be effectively controlled to maximize performance under the most stressful situations.

When trying to control fear, it is important for you to understand that it is a normal occurrence and that feeling it does not mean you are a coward or in some way "lacking guts." Openly discussing fear should be encouraged, in a manner that describes it as yet another challenge to be tackled. One scientific study showed that eight out of ten combat veterans felt that it is better to admit fear and discuss it openly before battle. The belief that "the man who knows he will be afraid and tries to get ready for it makes a better soldier" was shared by 58 percent of those surveyed.

Discussing fear has never been easy for SEALs, and probably never will be. Because they are almost all driven, Type-A personalities used to overcoming significant obstacles and performing much better than most "normal" men, SEALs are often reluctant to admit that they have any weaknesses, even those that they were born with. But SEAL leaders recognized that utilizing the information gained from various studies could enable them to enhance the performance of their operators as well as to help otherwise capable BUDS students graduate from the course.

Today, BUDS students are taught the Four Pillar Technique and the Rapid Response Technique as a way of maintaining their resolve and motivation in the face of stress and fear. Likewise, SEALs in operational units now understand that the body's reactions to situations associated with threat stress are as normal and predictable as when one is holding his breath while swimming underwater or when the body is subjected to prolonged cold that leads to hypothermia. SEALs now understand that what used to be attributed solely to "guts" is actually a man's ability to use his mind to anticipate and identify any situation that will trigger one or more of the body's physical responses to fear. Countering these responses early on will enable them to remain calm and effective on the battlefield.

Because SEALs have always engaged in challenging and realistic training, it was very easy for them to incorporate the concept of controlling fear into their training. SEALs are constantly exposed to training that replicates the tempo, stress, and physical and mental demands of actual combat situations, which provides them with almost unlimited opportunities to utilize these techniques to control their body's response to fear and threat stress. By now, these techniques are so well known and have proven so effective that they have become part of the individual SEAL's "tool box" and are hardly ever mentioned post-BUDS.

Now that you're aware of the findings of various research and scientific studies associated with the topic of fear and how to control it, I will offer a condensed summary of what all of the information means and how SEALs approach planned and unplanned events and situations that are associated with fear and threat stress. Remember, no matter how experienced a SEAL is or how proficient he becomes at controlling his body's responses to fear, the fact is that his body, like that of all humans, is hard-wired by millions of years of evolution to react in certain ways to fear and threat stress. These physical responses never go away; they remain with us as long as we live. A SEAL's ability to learn how to anticipate and control these predictable and ever-present responses is what enables him to keep a "cool head" in very dangerous situations and to perform at optimal levels.

Planned Events

It is obviously very easy to anticipate situations associated with fear and threat stress when you know in advance what is going to happen. A BUDS student will typically know what week or day a certain graded evolution is going to be conducted, such as Hell Week, timed running of the obstacle course, and specific graded runs and swims, and he's able to utilize the Four Pillar Technique to help him prepare mentally for these challenges.

The Four Pillar Technique

1. Goal Setting
2. Visualization
3. Self-Talk
4. Arousal Control

Unplanned Events

A common saying among military planners is "no battle plan survives the first shot." This means that even the best-laid plans can be almost immediately derailed once the "fog of war" occurs, and it occurs once the shooting starts and men begin to experience fear. SEALs understand this and are trained to expect the unexpected during operations. Thus, when confronted with sudden, unforeseen situations and events that bring forth fear and threat stress, they immediately and almost subconsciously revert to a modified version of the Four Pillar Technique that is referred to as the Rapid Response Technique. This technique enables SEALs to respond rapidly and effectively to unforeseen events and situations. It is effective not only when SEALs are in combat or training but also during their daily lives, when they are often confronted with unanticipated events and situations.

Rapid Response Technique

1. Arousal control.
2. Self-Talk.
3. Assess the situation relative to any threat to:
   - your personal safety and survival, and that of your teammates
   - accomplishing the mission
4. Consider appropriate courses of action and responses.
5. Take action.

6. Assess.

7. Repeat this cycle until the mission is accomplished or the situation is resolved.

In summary, the human body is programmed to respond to fear and threat stress in several predictable ways, and these responses can have a negative impact upon a person's performance during critical moments. Knowing that these physical responses will happen and understanding how to neutralize them is a critical factor in a SEAL being able to perform well in extremely dangerous and stressful situations.

SEALs continually practice this skill, and I believe that others desiring to become mentally tough and capable of performing well in conditions associated with great amounts of fear, stress, risk, and uncertainly should do the same. I encourage readers to practice the Four Pillar Technique and the Rapid Response Technique on a daily basis.

"Each time we face our fear, we gain strength, courage, and confidence in the doing."

—Theodore Roosevelt, 1901

Confidence

According to the Merriam-Webster's Collegiate Dictionary, confidence is defined as "a feeling or consciousness of one's powers or of reliance on one's circumstances" and "faith or belief that one will act in a right, proper, or effective way" and "the quality or state of being certain."

Based on these statements, it is clear that a person who possesses confidence in his or her abilities is a self-confident person, and self-confidence is a quality that lies at the very heart of this book, and is likely a quality that you desire to obtain or enhance. For the purposes of this chapter—and throughout the entire book—the terms *confidence* and *self-confidence* will be used interchangeably.

Why Self-Confidence Is So Important to a SEAL

Self-confidence is an essential quality for anyone attempting to become a Navy SEAL, and without it, it is almost impossible to complete BUDS successfully. It is also the foundation of the mental toughness that SEALs are famous for and exhibit on a daily basis during training and combat operations. It's been proven many times over that high level of confidence enable SEALs to establish high goals and to persevere while achieving them.

Confidence Is Contagious

Studies have shown that confident and successful people tend to associate personally and professionally with others possessing these same qualities. If you think about this for a moment, you will agree that, in all walks of life, business, academia, sports, and such, those who are operating at the highest levels of competence and achievement are typically surrounded by other high-level performers.

Remember when your parents, teachers, and coaches used to tell you things like "Birds of a feather flock together" and "You become who you associate with" when you were growing up? By now you likely agree with what they said, having seen both good and bad examples of these maxims played out in real life. This concept is also true within the SEAL community. Starting with the small number of classmates that survive BUDS and continue on to be assigned to operation units, SEALs are constantly surrounded by competent people, such as peers, seniors or subordinates. This in itself helps to perpetuate the "There ain't nothing a Frogman can't do" mentality that was established by the early forerunners of the current SEAL community and which remains at the very heart of each SEAL.

Confidence Is Visible

If confidence is contagious, it is also highly visible. If you ever get the chance to meet or observe a Navy SEAL, you will see that he carries himself with an aura of quiet confidence and bearing. While their personalities range from introvert to extrovert, SEALs literally walk and talk as if they are in complete control of themselves and the environment they are in.

While I cannot provide a specific list of things to look for regarding this visible confidence, you'll know it when you see it, and chances are you've already observed it in other high-performing individuals you know or have met throughout your life. Likewise, I doubt that you've ever observed a person who carried himself in a nervous, physically timid way and thought to yourself, *That guy looks like a winner!*

Indicators of Low Self-Confidence

We all know people who are lacking in self-confidence. My personal observations have shown that these people usually share some traits and behavior patterns.

- **Complaining.** People who spend most of their time complaining about things are often insecure and incapable of taking responsibility for themselves, their actions, specific situations, or outcomes. Complaining provides them with a means of diverting attention away from themselves. A popular saying among SEALs is that "Whiners can't be winners," and this is true in most walks of life.

- **Showing Off.** SEALs are highly competitive. They like to win, even when pitted against fellow SEALs. But it is considered bad form in the Teams for one to be a showoff, and this behavior is rarely seen and never tolerated. People with a tendency to show off are often insecure or lack confidence in their abilities, skills, or social standing. To compensate, they show off in a variety of ways to gain attention and the recognition they crave.

- **Addictions.** People lacking confidence often resort to destructive behavior, such as overeating or abuse of alcohol or drugs, in order to cope with their feelings of inadequacy.

- **Constant Need for Approval.** Some people need constant praise and assurances that they are doing well or they are liked and respected by others. At the heart of this is a lack of self-confidence. A person won't make it through BUDS if he needs *any* form of approval from the instructor staff, much less constant approval. And I dare say that, in most walks of life, people who need to be assured constantly that they are doing a good job will never reach the highest levels of achievement.

- **Self-Pity.** Once a man starts feeling sorry for himself, disappointment and defeat are soon to follow. Self-pity is what causes BUDS students to begin considering quitting, and eventually it's what causes them to ring the bell. I have never known a confident and competent person who felt sorry for himself in any situation, no matter how stressful or dangerous it was.

How to Develop Self-Confidence

Confidence is not something that just happens; it requires active nurturing and development over a period of time. The good news is that it does not require years to acquire higher levels of confidence, and in some cases a person can achieve significant results in a matter of days or weeks. The time frame varies greatly among individuals, and a lot depends on things such as a person's personal or professional situation and the experiences—good and bad—they've had over time.

SEALs typically do not have problems with a lack of confidence, but I realize that some reading this book might, and I want to convey what I feel is a sound method of developing confidence. This method is not meant to be a one-size-fits-all prescription that will guarantee a person will become more confident, but I think if studied and tailored to a person's specific situation and goals it can help greatly.

Here are three steps to get you going:

1. **Select Your Goal (personal or professional).** Chances are that you've already done this, but if not, define what it is that you desire to do—your goal or objective. This may be something you've tried to do in the past without success. It may be something that made you so nervous or fearful that you didn't even make an attempt. It may be something that you've seen others accomplish and thought to yourself *I wish I could do that.* The good news is that you can do it—but you need to decide to take action!

2. **Prepare Yourself.** This is the obvious next step after you've selected your goal. I've always enjoyed this aspect

of goal setting, actually doing the research and investigation into what it is going to take to achieve a goal or objective. Like many others, I find that learning about what is associated with achieving a goal is, in itself, a confidence builder. The content found in the **Preparation and Practice** and the **Setting Goals** chapters will help you formulate a plan of action.

3. **Visualize Success.** At this point in the book you should be aware of the importance of mental imagery and visualization relative to successfully achieving a goal or performing well under pressure. The fact that SEALs have included it as one of the pillars in the Four Pillar Technique should reinforce just how important it is that you see yourself achieving your goal, executing the specific skill or task, delivering a great performance or presentation to an audience, serving in a role or position within your company, losing weight—whatever it is that you desire to do.

I think you'll agree that people lacking confidence are more likely to believe that their success—or lack thereof—depends more on fate or on what others do to them or for them. They seem to have a feeling of hopelessness and resignation that the highest level of success, whatever that means to them personally, is out of reach and unattainable. This is not the mindset and attitude associated with people of success, and it is certainly not how Navy SEALs approach life. You have the ability to directly and immediately increase your level of self-confidence—you must believe this!

"If you have no confidence in self, you are twice defeated in the race of life. With confidence, you have won even before you have started."

—Cicero, 50 BC

Setting Goals

The fact that you are reading this book implies that you have goals related to your personal or professional life. Whatever these goals are, they should be clearly stated in a way that enables you to assess your progress toward reaching them. There are many techniques used for this, and almost all of them, if executed properly, will help you achieve your goals. One popular technique is called the SMART Goals Method, and it has been used by many people for several decades. It is a simple and easy-to-learn method, and I encourage you to give it a try when setting and refining your list of goals.

The SMART Goals Method

The SMART goal-setting approach involves a goal that's specific, measurable, attainable, relevant, and time-bound.

Specific Goals

This term stresses the need for clearly defined, specific goals instead of broadly defined, general ones. This means that a goal must be clear and unambiguous, without unnecessary adjectives and "fluff." For goals to be specific, they must illustrate exactly what is expected, why is it important, who's involved, where is it going to happen, and which attributes are important.

A specific goal will usually answer these questions:

- What? What do I want to accomplish?
- Why? Specific reasons, purpose, and benefits of accomplishing the goal.
- Who? Everyone that will be directly or indirectly involved in accomplishing the goal.
- Where? Identify specific, relevant locations, if appropriate.

Measurable Goals

This term stresses the need for clearly defined criteria that can be used for measuring progress toward goal accomplishment. Simply put, all goals must be able to be isolated, defined, and measured. Without constant measurement and evaluation of one's progress toward the accomplishment of a goal, it is often difficult to determine if you're making forward strides or if you're treading water. Most planning experts agree that the majority of people and organizations that fail to reach their goals do so because they did not apply an adequate form of measurement to keep track of their progress.

A measurable goal will usually answer questions such as

- How much?
- How many?
- How will I know when it is accomplished?

Attainable Goals

This term stresses the importance of setting goals that are both realistic and attainable. Throughout this book there has been a heavy emphasis on the concept of a person stretching beyond his or her real and perceived limitations to accomplish his or her goals. Most goals of a significant value are in fact "stretch goals" that require the mental toughness and resolve to push through barriers, but the fact remains that they must be attainable. Some people set goals that are aggressive or challenging to the point that they become unrealistic or unattainable. The micro-task concept is an effective technique when setting attainable goals. For example, instead of a person stating they will lose 20 pounds, they should consider stating that they will lose 2 pounds per week for 10 weeks.

An attainable goal will usually answer these questions:

- Have others accomplished it, or is there a realistic opportunity to accomplish it?
- How can the goal be accomplished?
- Do I have access to the appropriate knowledge, tools, and time required to accomplish this goal?

Relevant Goals

This term stresses the importance of selecting goals that truly matter to what a person wants to accomplish. A mid-level manager's goal of losing 20 pounds by Christmas may be relevant to his personal life, but it might have no impact at all on his professional goal of becoming a vice president within his company. It is imperative that you clearly define the goal you truly wish to accomplish, and ensure that every other action you take to achieve it directly relates to that goal.

A relevant goal can answer yes to these questions:

- If I accomplish this, will my most important goals be reached?
- Is this the right time to do this?
- Is accomplishing this goal relevant to my chances of success toward accomplishing my ultimate goal?

Time-bound Goals

This term stresses the critical importance of assigning a time frame to all goals. Aligning a goal with specific dates and time-related milestones instills a sense of urgency and accountability among the people involved in accomplishing it. It also enables the measurement aspect of the SMART Goal Method. Setting time parameters and due dates is very helpful in ensuring that progress toward accomplishing a goal is not overtaken by inevitable emergencies and issues that occur in everyone's lives. When such things happen, having a timeline enables you to quickly assess how much your plan has been affected, and can help you set a new course to regain momentum and get back on track.

A time-bound goal will usually answer these questions:

- When will the goal be reached?
- What are the intermediate due dates assigned to micro-tasks and smaller objectives?
- What progress must be achieved by next week, 6 weeks from now, in 90 days?

I'm quite sure that everyone reading this book has a desire to achieve something of significant value, and they have realized that to do so will require a level of mental toughness and self-confidence that exceeds that which they already possess. However, as beneficial as acquiring the qualities that increase your mental toughness could be that effort won't yield optimal results if the goals and objectives themselves are not well thought out and clearly defined. The SMART Goal Method has worked well for me, and it has worked well for many SEALs and other SOF operators. It has also been used to great effect by countless people in professions ranging from the business world to the medical field to academia to sports. It is a proven method, and I encourage you to use it.

Finally, I want to remind you of an old saying that you've probably heard sometime in your lifetime: "If you fail to plan, you are planning to fail!" These are words to live by indeed.

"Strategy without tactics is the slowest route to victory. Tactics without strategy is the noise before defeat."

—Sun Tzu, 512 BC

Preparation and Practice

Mental toughness is based on confidence, and confidence stems from a person's unshakeable faith in his or her ability to perform a skill or task. Obviously, such ability and competence in any skill or task are attained through training and practice. There have been numerous research studies conducted on the attainment of competence at the expert level, and I will cover some of the findings of these studies in this chapter.

Dr. Anders Ericsson, considered by many to be the world's leading researcher of the topic of high performance, believes that the key factor in the attainment of expert-level skill is a person's willingness to work hard and to engage in what he calls "deliberate practice."

Ericsson has stated: "People believe that because expert performance is qualitatively different from normal performance the expert performer must be endowed with characteristics qualitatively different from those of normal adults. We agree that expert performance is qualitatively different from normal performance and even that expert performers have characteristics and abilities that are qualitatively different from or at least outside the range of those of normal adults. However, we deny that these differences are immutable, that is, due to innate talent. Only a few exceptions, most notably height, are genetically prescribed. Instead, we argue that the differences between expert performers and normal adults reflect a life-long period of deliberate effort to improve performance in a specific domain."

As you can see, Dr. Ericsson does not support the mantra that most of us grew up hearing—and believing—that essentially stated, - individuals who are very good at certain skills possess some kind of genetic advantage that the rest of us "ordinary" people do not. His research, and that of others, concludes that, while top performers certainly possess qualities, traits, and habits that are the foundation of their success, none of these attributes are beyond the reach of any other human being. I've mentioned previously that many incredibly gifted athletes and physical specimens often fail to successfully complete BUDS, while other far less physically capable men do. I know several SEALs who were told by others that there was no way they'd be able to complete BUDS and make it to the Teams. Rather than be discouraged by being told they were too small, not strong enough, or too slow to be able to gut it through BUDS, these guys simply went out, attacked the course, and became SEALs. Perhaps you've heard similar things said about your ability to do something or attain certain goals.

One of Dr. Ericsson's fundamental findings was that becoming an expert at any skill has less to do with how much practice a person engages in and more with the quality of practice. His results show, instead of our parents and coaches telling us that "Practice makes perfect", they should have said...

"Perfect practice makes perfect!"

His research also found that most high performers broke down the skills they wanted to excel at into smaller chunks, or micro-tasks, and focused on improving their proficiency at them, which in turn led to improved execution of the macro-task or skill. Additionally, he found that experts habitually practiced their skills under a variety of realistic and increasingly challenging conditions.

Much of the findings of Dr. Ericsson's research aligns with the overall attitude and approach used by BUDS students and SEALs alike. To become good at something, you have to practice it, and practicing it perfectly under a variety of increasingly challenging conditions is a sure path to exceptional performance. This should be empowering to anyone who desires to become an expert or a high performer at any skill or task, and should help them understand that the only thing standing between them and the attainment of their goals is their own willingness to commit to hard work.

This brings me to the main message of this chapter, which is that you will indeed "play as you practice," and when it comes time to perform under stressful and high-pressure conditions, you will always revert, physically and mentally, to the level at which you practiced and trained. SEALs spend a lot of time learning how to conduct close-quarter battle (CQB) operations, which include moving and shooting from one room to another in buildings that contain enemy combatants and civilians. Suffice it to say that it requires a great amount of proficiency with various weapons to be able to quickly identify and shoot the bad guys without hitting the innocent civilians standing next to them. SEALs practice CQB relentlessly and demand of themselves an extremely high level of competence and accuracy. They focus on perfect practice, and this typically leads to perfect or near-perfect shooting.

This kind of practice creates a form of muscle memory, and your brain begins to recognize various physical and mental patterns, which promotes faster and more efficient movement and clarity of thought over time. The more you engage in perfect practice the easier it will become for you to perform specific skills and tasks well under even the most stressful conditions.

I have successfully applied the principle of perfect practice to most aspects of my life, personal and professional, and it has worked well for me. I've learned over time that the key to continuous high performance is continuous perfect practice. I want to share with you some things that I've learned over time and have helped me acquire knowledge and proficiency.

- **Read.** Chances are that whatever skill or task you desire to become proficient at has been the subject of books, articles, and research studies. Reading such information enables you to absorb the lessons learned by many and will significantly enhance your ability to rapidly elevate your level of performance. Reading about the experiences of others can help you avoid making the same mistakes they made. Every SEAL and special operator that I've ever known had an almost insatiable thirst for knowledge, and almost all were voracious readers. There's an old saying: "Experience is the best teacher, but it is also the most expensive!" I cannot emphasize this too strongly: **START READING NOW!**

- **Learn from the best.** Much can be gained from observing people who have already achieved what you desire to achieve. Study their background—education, training, and experience—which led them to being successful. Try to determine if there are common traits, characteristics, and skills that these top performers possess and you'd probably need to possess to match their level of success. If possible, observe them while they practice and perform the skills and tasks that you are focused on, and try to identify anything, any pattern or nuance, that might provide some insight you can use to your advantage. During my military career I learned a lot by interacting with members of the British Special Air Service and operators from various Special Forces and Marine Force Recon units. I've found that almost all top-level performers are very willing to share their experiences and advice with others, and I encourage you to consider approaching someone you admire and asking them for advice and guidance.

- **Seek expert feedback.** Ask a knowledgeable, competent person to observe you during practice or while you are performing and provide you with honest, unvarnished feedback. Seek out those who will level with you and tell you what you are doing well, what you are doing poorly, and what you should do in order to elevate your game. Be willing to hear the truth, even if it stings a bit.

- **Focus on winning.** Your focus should be on winning, not losing. So many people let the fear of failure overwhelm them, and this has a very damaging effect on their confidence. The guys that start BUDS thinking that they won't make it ... *don't make it.* Those who begin BUDS with an "I will die before I quit" mentality are the guys who are standing tall on graduation day. Practice like a winner. Anticipate mistakes and unexpected situations and deal with them. Do not let the fear of losing or not performing well dominate your brain's "hard drive"—***THINK LIKE A WINNER!***

- Whatever your goals are, know that attaining them is going to require a lot of perfect practice. If you are willing to commit the time and energy required, there's no reason why you can't achieve anything you set your mind to!

"We are what we repeatedly do. Excellence, then, is not an act but a habit."

*—***Aristotle, 350 BC**

Physical Training

Chances are you purchased this book because you want to improve your mental toughness. Most don't set out with the intention to match the physical capabilities of Navy SEALs, which for many is an unrealistic goal. The good news is that anyone, regardless of age and physical condition, is capable of developing mental toughness on the same level as that possessed by SEALs.

So, what of intense physical training and its role in the development of mental toughness? Is there a correlation between the two? I think so, and numerous research studies conducted within the military and sports populations validate my belief. Individuals in both of these groups are often required to perform at a high level under very stressful physical and psychological conditions; and it has been proven beyond doubt that those who have repeatedly practiced under similar conditions become more adept at handling the stresses and pressures, and, most important, they perform well when it counts.

If you understand the type of missions that SEALs are asked to execute on a routine basis, you can see that there is a need for these men to possess exceptional mental toughness and resolve in very dangerous situations. History has proven that the only way to ensure a man will be able to perform successfully in such situations is to evaluate his performance under similar conditions in a training environment. For the SEAL community, this is what BUDS is used for, to impose challenging and, at times, seemingly impossible mental and physical demands on the students and to find those possessing the raw aptitude to serve as SEALs.

I think it is safe to say that almost all SEALs will agree that BUDS was far more physically difficult than anything they ever had to do while operating in combat. Most will also say that, while they've been tired and cold during combat operations, they've never been as physically exhausted or as cold as they were during BUDS, especially during Hell Week. I don't know any SEAL who won't readily admit that on more than one occasion, when times got tough, he reflected on BUDS and the fact that he made it through such a challenge and there was no reason why he couldn't get through the one he was currently facing.

I think there is a high probability that the readers of this book are already somewhat familiar with the fact that Navy SEALs are the products of an exceptionally rigorous physical-training program (BUDS). They also may believe that this is the major factor in the development of the mental toughness demonstrated by these highly trained warriors. While they are correct in thinking this, they mistakenly also think that physical training such as that found at BUDS is the only route to SEAL-like mental toughness. I want to emphasize to all readers, including those with significant physical limitations, which intense physical training is indeed one method used in the development of mental toughness, but it is not the only one. There are millions of people in this world that possess exceptional mental toughness and would never be considered physically capable of serving as a Navy SEAL. This is a fact, and it should encourage and reassure you that, regardless of your current level of physical ability, as long as you have a functioning mind and a desire to develop enhanced levels of mental toughness and self-confidence, you absolutely can.

Throughout my life I have met countless mentally tough people, of all ages and backgrounds, who would probably not survive a single day at BUDS because they simply do not possess the physical ability to do so. At the risk of repeating myself, I want you to know that, if you are seeking to increase your level of mental toughness, you can do so even if you are not capable of performing at high levels of physical effort or are limited to the point where you cannot engage in any type of physical activity. All that is required to become mentally tough is the desire to do so and a mind that is willing to take charge and make it happen!

Obviously, I am a huge fan of intense physical training, and I believe that it played a major role in my personal and physical development. I think it had a huge impact upon the success I enjoyed during my military career, both while training and serving in combat operations. If you do a Google search for *mental toughness*, you will see many articles and stories about people doing almost impossible things in various situations and environments that have nothing to do with the military or high-level athletics. You'll also notice that there is a huge number of books, training programs, seminars, and the like available on the commercial market that are associated with acquiring mental toughness and self-confidence. Most of them have nothing to do with physical training other than the fact that almost all of them encourage a person to engage in exercise as a way of pursuing good health and controlling stress.

I certainly encourage anyone capable of engaging in a physical-training program to do so. But I also know that many people reading this book are well into their "second half" of life, and I'd be negligent if I failed to advise them to be realistic as they contemplate beginning an exercise program. For many, I suspect that the next physical-exercise session they engage in will be their first in many years, perhaps even their first ever. If this is true, I want you to do two things. First, make sure you see a medical doctor to ensure that you are cleared to begin physical training. Second, I advise you to be realistic when selecting what kind of physical training you will engage in. Be honest with yourself regarding your current physical condition and health, and participate in a realistic and safe training program that helps you make steady progress toward your goals.

For those who are already in good physical condition and are currently engaging in physical training, I advise you to reflect on your goals and whether or not you are making progress toward them. As stated earlier, I am a huge fan of physical training—some would say that I am obsessed with it—and I train at a level at which men younger than I cannot. If you are one who is medically and physically capable of safely engaging in some of the more intense physical-training regimens that are popular these days—Cross Fit, P90x, Insanity, for example—then by all means do so. If you aspire to become a Navy SEAL, there are several very good fitness programs, books, and DVDs created by former SEALs that are available for purchase online.

It is important to remember that physical training is a great way to obtain and maintain good health, and all else being equal, a healthy body serves as the foundation for a healthy, confident, and mentally tough mind.

"When health is absent, wisdom cannot reveal itself, art cannot manifest, strength cannot fight, wealth becomes useless, and intelligence cannot be applied."

—Herophilus, 300 BC

The SEAL Mindset

While writing this book, I maintained a notebook in which I recorded random thoughts and ideas concerning the topic of mental toughness and other issues related to the Navy SEALs. Over time, I had created a collection of notes that listed some of the dominant personality traits and attitudes that I had observed in the many SEALs I had known during the course of my military career. I think these notes are worth mentioning.

SEALs Maintain a High Belief in Their Training

As mentioned earlier, a key ingredient of mental toughness is confidence, and confidence comes from several sources. One source of a Navy SEAL's confidence is his training, starting with BUDS, continuing to the subsequent SEAL Qualification Training program, and then to the almost nonstop unit and individual training he receives throughout his time in an operational unit.

SEALs truly believe that they have passed the toughest special-operations selection course in the world and that they have received the best tactical and technical training to enable them to accomplish any assigned mission or task. As a result, SEALs exude an aura of quiet confidence in all they do. They believe they are fully capable, mentally and physically, to achieve success in anything they attempt. This belief is the foundation in the development of their self-confidence.

SEALs See Themselves as Winners

SEALs are no different than other high-performing individuals in various professions in that they have a very positive self-image. Psychological studies show that the men who successfully graduate from BUDS possess a high level of competitiveness and an almost insatiable desire to win. This desire to win, or "fire in the gut" as it is often referred to in the SEAL community, is essentially what enables a BUDS student to stick with the program when others are quitting.

Once assigned to a SEAL team, these newly trained operators are surrounded by and interact daily with several dozen more-experienced SEALs, all of whom possess similar attitudes and personality traits, the most dominant of which is that all SEALs see themselves first and foremost as winners. This "tribe of winners" invariably produces a warrior that believes he can not only successfully accomplish any assigned mission or task but that he can do it better and faster than anyone else, even a fellow SEAL.

SEALs Focus on Why They Will Succeed

Because SEALs are extremely competitive, they tend to view almost any task as a contest that must not only be won but won in a fashion that exceeds that of previous winners. Whether it is a timed distance run pitting them against their teammates, a graded run through the CQB shooting house, or taking down a gas-oil platform far out to sea, SEALs are always competing, and when competing, they always believe they are capable of winning.

Since their initial training at BUDS is difficult and so few successfully complete it, graduating from the course promotes a huge degree of self-confidence among SEALs, and they typically use this asset to help them focus on the task at hand, all the while thinking of the many reasons why they are about to succeed at it and once again be a winner. Most SEALs leverage their past successes—such as the training they've endured or the preparation they've put in for a specific event, challenge, or mission—as reasons why they will undoubtedly succeed again.

SEALs Use Positive Self-Talk

As stated in a previous chapter, the human mind is engaged in an almost constant stream of self-talk, and SEALs are taught to control this internal conversation and ensure it is of a positive nature. Studies have shown that individuals with the ability to consciously and quickly eliminate or minimize negative self-talk and focus on positive, inspirational self-talk tend to perform more effectively during periods of stress. When engaging in self-talk, many SEALs use statements such as "I'm going to have a great run" or "I'm going to shoot my best scores ever this morning" or "I've done this so many times before, I got this!" and other positive and motivating thoughts that foster confidence.

SEALs Don't Let Doubts Rule

Doubt destroys confidence—this is a fact that has been verified in countless studies. It is also a fact that individuals who are perfectionists, overly driven, or pessimistic are often more prone to dwell on doubt to the degree that it diminishes or destroys their performance when it matters most. Very few SEALs are pessimists, but many do possess tendencies of a perfectionist nature and all of them are highly motivated, which could make them more susceptible to succumbing to doubt if left unchecked.

With this in mind, SEALs are taught to face any doubts they may be having head-on and quickly dismiss them, and instead focus on positive self-talk. They are adept at removing doubt from their conscious mind by filling it instead with thoughts that will ultimately lead to desired levels of performance and accomplishment of the mission. In other words, SEALs are human beings, and they experience doubt like any other human. The difference between a SEAL and an untrained individual is that the SEAL is fully aware of doubt when it occurs and they immediately take action to counter this doubt. The SEAL works to restore his mind to a positive state, which is more conducive to optimal performance.

SEALs Think, Feel, and Project Confidence

Most Navy SEALs are optimists by nature, and this enables them to see opportunities where others might see obstacles and challenges too difficult to overcome. Fueling this optimism is the extensive training and personal development that all SEALs undergo, which produces in them an unshakeable confidence in their abilities to overcome any challenge, big or small.

If you've ever been around a group of SEALs, you likely observed that their very posture and body language projects an aura of confidence. It's difficult to explain or illustrate what I mean by this, but if you've seen it, you know what I mean. SEALs are supremely confident in their training and abilities as well as that of their teammates, and even without speaking to them, a casual observer will quickly be able to ascertain that there is something different about them.

SEALs Anticipate Success

SEALs are taught to use visualization techniques prior to engaging in an event or during the pursuit of a goal. They mentally rehearse their actions and see themselves performing the various steps, procedures, techniques, and tactics that will be required to successfully complete the mission. For example, a SEAL will visualize himself exiting the submarine and proceeding toward the area targeted for infiltration during a night lock-out; or fast roping down from a helicopter onto the roof of a building occupied by enemy forces.

Whatever the task or operation at hand, SEALs approach it with an **"I GOT THIS!"** mentality, and in their minds they see themselves performing well throughout each step or phase of the upcoming event or operation.

SEALs Prepare Strategies and Game Plans

Most highly competent, successful people develop strategies, plans, and tactics to be used in the pursuit of goals and objectives. SEALs do the same as they attempt to control as many factors as possible when devising a plan of attack or course of action that will lead to successfully completing a mission or assigned task. Beginning with their training at BUDS and continuing throughout their assignment to an operational unit, SEALs are expected to think on their feet and make rapid decisions when necessary.

When time permits, SEALs engage in very detailed planning for missions and operations, utilizing all of their experience and skills to produce a game plan that stacks the deck in their favor regarding the successful accomplishment of the assigned mission. This is made possible by exploiting many years of SEAL experience that have been consolidated into various standard operating procedures (SOPs) for practically every task, tactic, and technique that a SEAL will ever be required to execute in training or during combat operations.

These SOPs are memorized and practiced relentlessly by every member of a SEAL team, and cover everything from how to conduct a nighttime free-fall parachute insertion to how to employ specific weapon systems to the brevity codes used when communicating with each other and higher headquarters during operations, and so on. The goal of all of this planning is to control that which can be controlled and, to the extent possible, leave nothing to chance.

SEALs Anticipate the Unexpected

Despite being exceptionally adept at planning and shaping the actions that will occur during the execution of a mission, SEALs operate under the philosophy that no battle plan survives the first shot, which means that even the best-conceived plans often fall victim to unforeseen events and rapidly changing situations.

Knowing this, SEALs anticipate that there will be spontaneous and, often, multiple obstacles facing them during a mission, and they remain mentally flexible and ready to respond with timely decisions to counter them. In fact, they practice this skill continuously during training so they can maintain and refine their ability to cope with the unexpected, no matter what it is, and remain focused on the most important thing: successful accomplishment of the assigned mission. Knowing that they have acquired this skill is in itself a confidence builder and a significant part of the mental toughness associated with SEALs.

SEALs Have Patience

When most people think of the Navy SEALs, they think of physically strong, mentally tough men of action. While this is certainly an accurate view of these special warriors, most would probably be surprised at how critical it is that a SEAL possess the ability to exercise patience when appropriate. Whether it is while learning how to operate and employ highly sophisticated and classified satellite communications equipment, planning a complex mission, or when in actual combat operations, a SEAL must have the ability to sense when being patient is the best thing he can do to ensure the success of any given mission.

Combat operations rarely unfold as planned, and in addition to reacting effectively to any unforeseen tactical developments that surface, it is essential that SEALs also exercise patience and caution in doing so, lest they react too quickly or in a manner that enables the enemy to gain an advantage or that otherwise endangers the successful accomplishment of the mission or assigned tasks.

SEALs have many other positive attributes and personality traits, but those listed above are what I feel are the main factors that result in the mental toughness, confidence, and competence associated with these warriors.

NAVY SEAL MINDSET

Chances of Success

%	
0%	I won't.
10%	I can't.
20%	I wish I could.
30%	I don't know how.
40%	I want to.
50%	I think I may.
60%	I may.

How most people think.

How Navy SEALs think.

%	
70%	I think I can.
80%	I can.
90%	I will.
100%	I did.

"The Spartans do not ask how many the enemy are, but where they are."

—Agis II, 400 BC

SEAL Interviews

While conducting research for this book, I spoke with many former and current SEALs about the topic of mental toughness. I took the audio recordings and notes made during these interviews and discussions and edited them into an easily read format. I think you'll find their thoughts and comments quite interesting.

John – Senior Chief Petty Officer

When Lars contacted me and asked if I'd agree to an interview on the topic of mental toughness as related to my time serving in the Teams, I initially declined his request. I had no problem with the fact that he was writing a book on the topic, but I felt that such a book was unnecessary for any young man aspiring to become a SEAL. I'm an old-school frogman, and back when I first became interested in the SEAL community there were no books, videos, or websites available—the internet had not yet been invented—to help me prepare for BUDS. I was simply told to report for duty on a certain date in the best possible physical condition. I'll be honest—I don't like the fact that so much inside information is publicly available these days for SEAL candidates. I think it provides them with an edge that lessens some of the impact of the weeding-out aspect of the course. I know many SEALs do not agree with my views on this, but I don't think it has been beneficial to the SEAL community as a whole to have so much of our training program and methods available to the public.

About a month after I declined the initial request for an interview, Lars called me again and explained that the book he was writing was more for civilians and less for SEAL candidates. He told me that it really was aimed at ordinary people who desired to learn more about how to become mentally tougher or increase their self-confidence. He said that he thought his book would be of benefit to readers ranging from teens to people in their 60s, and working in various professions—Wall Street stock traders, firemen, law-enforcement officers, business leaders, young college graduates in the early stage of their careers, people in sales jobs, lawyers, doctors, people trying to lose weight or cope with tough personal situations, etc. I realized that he was right, and that almost anyone would benefit from hearing a SEAL's perspective on what those of us in the Teams almost take for granted: the mindset and attitude that, however difficult or dangerous a situation or challenge is, SEALs truly believe they can come overcome it and do better than anyone else on this earth!

Perhaps things have changed, but when I went through BUDS, we didn't receive any special training on mental toughness or self-confidence. In fact, it was just the opposite; the instructors did everything possible to destroy our ability to believe they could survive the course and become a member of the Teams! It was the training itself, day after day, that made us wage a battle in our minds, asking ourselves how much longer we wanted to keep subjecting ourselves to those torture sessions supervised by sadists and lunatics!

I saw many people quit at BUDS who had all the necessary attributes and traits required to serve as a SEAL except one—the ability to remain mentally focused when faced with continuous and very stressful challenges and situations. I also saw many make it through the course who were physically quite ordinary. However, they kept going day after day as if at some point they simply arrived to a mental state that basically said, "Others have made it through this course and I can too!" That's what I did; I told myself that no matter how bad things got for me, the fact was that many hundreds of guys just like me had made it through BUDS, and that on graduation day some members of my class would be graduating from the course and there was no reason I could not be among them!

During my time in the Teams I obviously served with many very tough characters with personalities ranging from quiet, almost introverted guys to those who were loud and outgoing. The common denominator among these men was the fact that they all had a very strong, competitive personality and they really enjoyed competing against challenges most others found too difficult or even impossible to overcome. I think this kind of competitive personality requires one to have a great deal of self-confidence, and I do think that it's a quality that can be developed over time through training and experience. Even in the Teams, many of the younger, less experienced guys often don't exhibit the same level of mental toughness possessed by SEALs old enough to be their fathers. I've seen many a young SEAL, confident from his recent victory at BUDS; grow far more confident and self-assured as he was continually exposed to very difficult and dangerous training environments. SEALs are always competing with themselves and their teammates. I think the fact that they enjoy being "graded" every single day by their peers results in very sharp minds that simply refuse to accept the slightest possibility that they won't win the next event, be it a 5-mile beach run, a 5,000-meter night swim in the open ocean, a shooting event, or even a combat operation.

When I was in high school, I read a quote that was attributed to Henry Ford that stated, "Whether you think you can or you think you can't—you're right." That statement had a very profound impact on me as a high-school athlete, and I achieved honors as a football player that far surpassed my actual athletic ability and skill at the game. The bottom line was that, while I was small for a linebacker, I approached each play with the mindset that any person I hit would have to be carried off the field. I was that "small guy" who managed to hit much bigger running backs so hard that they often had to leave the game, not because they were physically injured but because they simply did not want to take the pain associated with running in my direction.

To those reading this book, I'd say that history is full of examples of people achieving things they were supposed to be incapable of, and that you should never allow anyone (including yourself!) to tell you that you can't do something that you desire to do. I think if you research whatever your goal is and study people who have already achieved it, you'll find that there are many who have the same or even fewer qualifications, experience, and ability than you currently possess, yet they somehow managed to succeed.

Alan – Petty Officer

I went through BUDS in the late '60s, when America was involved in Vietnam. Like almost all of my classmates, whether or not they were assigned to a SEAL Team or a UDT, I eventually served in Vietnam.

Lars has told me that many of those being interviewed for this book are relating some of their BUDS experiences as a way of conveying their thoughts on the topic of mental toughness, confidence, etc., and I think it is appropriate for me to do the same.

I went through BUDS in an era in which little was known about the UDT/SEAL community, and even less was known about our training. I suspect there were far less formal "rules" back then than there are today, and perhaps the instructor cadre may have had a bit more latitude regarding what a class did on any given training day. I say this not to denigrate the BUDS of today; in fact, from everything that I've heard and seen, the course is in many ways better, and in some ways even tougher than the BUDS I managed to survive.

By now, you probably know that SEALs are highly competitive people, and as individuals and an entire community, they place a high value on being able to conquer any and all challenges they may face. In the SEAL culture, winning and accomplishing the mission at hand are to be done at all costs. Right from the first day of BUDS the instructors began to instill upon us that winners would be rewarded and losers would be punished.

Additionally, you must realize that in BUDS, at least at that time, the instructors considered just about everything we did to be a graded event. The cleanliness of our barracks, how we folded and placed our towels on the end of our bunks, how closely we shaved that morning, how we laced our boots, falling out in formation so we could run to the chow hall, staging our boats and equipment exactly as instructed (placement of the paddles, life vests, etc., inside the small rubber boats we carried), how quickly we completed the obstacle course as a team—everything, every task and detail, no matter how small or mundane, was subject to the scrutiny of the instructors. This offered the potential for individuals and boat teams to be declared winners or losers at just about any time during a training day.

During the initial weeks of BUDS the boat team I was assigned to did not perform well during the numerous and continuous graded and competitive events that pitted one team against another. We never won or placed high in a single event; in fact, we almost always finished last or very close to last. We became highly visible to the instructors, and they labeled us the "Commies" and referred to us as such nonstop as they mercilessly punished us for being losers. I can still vividly remember lying on the beach with the rest of my boat team after we finished last in a timed distance run, completely soaked and coated with sand (literally like a chicken leg coated with bread crumbs), doing flutter kicks and hearing some sarcastic instructor saying over a bullhorn, "We know who you are, Boat Team Six, you're not fooling us! We know you were sent here by the Kremlin to infiltrate the Teams. It won't work, because we are going to kill every single one of you commie bastards!"

I can't explain why my boat team did not perform well. It contained the same mix of students as the other teams did, yet for some reason we just could not manage to hit our stride at anything we did, be it running, swimming, the obstacle course, or doing calisthenics on the grinder. Nothing we did was good enough to place us in the top half of the boat teams. Because we were "losers," we were being punished on a nearly continuous basis, and I suspect on any given day we were doing far more pushups, flutter kicks, mountain climbers, and sprints to the surf so we could then roll around in the sand than the vast majority of our class. The members of my boat team began to tire, and though none of us actually mentioned it, we were being thrashed so badly by the instructors that our morale and resolve were affected. Even worse, we were beginning each training day already exhausted.

One day, as our class began running to the obstacle course with our boats held over our heads, an instructor told my boat team to stand fast and await instructions. As we watched the rest of our class run down the road, none of us said anything, but we all knew that whatever was about to happen to us was not going to be good. An instructor appeared and told us to pick up our boat and follow him. We did so, and noticed we were running toward the bay. As we got closer, we saw that there were a few instructors already standing on the beach next to a military ambulance. When our team arrived near the ambulance, we were told to stop running but to keep the boat in the upright position. An instructor approached us and said, "Today is the day, commies. Today is the day that we finally get rid of your sorry asses. I guarantee you that by the end of today this entire boat team will either be dead or it will be dropped from the class. Now, get your asses out in the water and report to Instructor Jones!"

As we looked out at the water, we saw that there were already two small rubber boats positioned next to each other, and it was obvious that there were a couple of instructors in each of them. We paddled out to them, and one of the instructors began talking to us with a bullhorn. He said that we should remove our life vests and "prepare for water torture"—whatever that meant!

He told us to get into the water, which we did, and as we treaded water next to the boat he was in, he showed us what looked like a 10-pound plate used for weightlifting. Attached to it were two lengths of rope about five feet long. He had two of these weights with ropes attached, and announced that "today's evolution is underwater knot tying" and said that we were to dive to the ocean floor, find the weight, and tie whatever knot he directed us to tie and bring it back up to the surface for him and the other instructor to inspect.

At this point he said "Bowline" and heaved both weights into the water, but separated by about 20 feet or so in order to cause our boat team to split up. We immediately split up at the direction of the boat team leader—a petty officer—and searched for the weights so we could tie bowlines on the ropes and bring them to the instructors.

This task proved to be quite difficult to accomplish, and we struggled to coordinate our efforts as a team. Remember, we had no dive masks, fins, or any other equipment, and worse, we had not expected this event and we were all quite confused and disoriented. Our initial attempt at performing this task took about 10 minutes to accomplish, and when we handed the instructor the weights, he immediately stated that the bowlines were both tied incorrectly, threw them into the water, and said "Square knot."

I think you can tell where this story is headed. We repeated this sequence nonstop for about an hour, which proved to be exhausting. Everyone was getting very tired.

At this point the instructor told us that if we could manage to tie three successive knots correctly, he would allow us to grab on to our boat, which was tied to his, and rest for a while instead of having to tread water. It may not seem like much to those reading this, but the thought of such a "reward" was quite attractive at that time.

As you might have predicted, our first two knots were deemed acceptable, but the instructor told us that one of the third knots was incorrect. He then ordered us to tread water and began asking us random questions, such as "What state is Instructor Smith from?" and "What year was Master Chief Johnson's car made?" If we answered incorrectly, we were ordered to dive down to the bottom of the ocean and bring up some sand in each hand. This went on for about 30 minutes, and then we returned to the knot-tying exercise, with similar dismal results and punishment.

I could tell by looking at the position of the sun that it was now midmorning, which meant that we had been at this for nearly four hours. By this time, some members of our boat team were beginning to show visible signs of being near the breaking point mentally, and were probably thinking of quitting. To be honest, I was one of them!

Out of all the physical tasks and harassment I had faced at BUDS so far, for some reason, this particular "torture session" was affecting me in a very bad way. I was angry at the instructors and was tired of being labeled a "commie" and a loser.

To make things worse, the instructor then informed us that he had spoken with the lead instructor via the radio he had in his boat and was told that this evolution could only be secured if someone quit. We were silent as we treaded water and bobbed up, and I knew that every one of us was hoping that someone would swim over to the instructor's boat and quit.

After about 10 seconds of silence, the instructor threw both weights into the ocean and said "Bowline." We scrambled to retrieve the weights and tie the knots correctly for another 30 minutes or so, all the while hearing the instructors tormenting us on the bullhorns, calling us communist agents and encouraging us to quit so we could all get back to the barracks for hot showers and donuts.

At some point the instructor called us over to the side of his boat and told us to grab the rope that ran the length of the boat. We did so, and he began talking to us with the bullhorn, stating that the lead instructor had just told him that the evolution could now be secured only if two students quit within the next five minutes; otherwise, the evolution would continue on throughout the day and into the night. The instructor "pleaded" with us via the bullhorn, saying things like "Come on, people, we can end this right now. None of you really want to be a frogman, let's head back in so we can clean up and get warm" and "Be smart, quit now. Even if you make it through BUDS, you'll get sent to Vietnam. Do you really want to die?" and other motivating words of encouragement! He then threw both weights into the water and said "Square knot," which caused us to immediately scramble to retrieve the weights.

As my half of the boat team was searching for one of the weights, I noticed one of the guys swim away from us and head toward the surface. I knew that he was quitting, and to be honest, I was hoping that someone else would also quit so we could end this torture session. When we surfaced with our weight, I noticed that there were two members of our boat team sitting in our boat. I felt great knowing that we were finally going to be done with this bullshit.

The instructor called us over to the side of the boat, and I think we were all expecting to hear him tell us that the water-torture evolution was secured and to head back to the beach. Thank God, I thought to myself, because I knew that I was physically exhausted and could not endure much more of this. The instructor informed us that he had bad news and said that, even though two students had quit, the second one did not quit within the five-minute time limit. He then threw both weights into the water and said "Bowline."

After three or four long seconds of thought, I dove toward where I thought the weight was, and with a couple of my mates, tied the knot and surfaced with it. Once at the surface, I saw that there were now four students in our boat, which meant there were only three of us left.

The instructor looked at our knots and deemed one of them defective. He threw the weights into the water and said "Square knot." The three of us found the first weight, put a square knot on the rope, and gave it to the instructor, and then went after the second weight and completed that knot. We repeated this sequence four or five more times over the next 30 minutes or so, all the while hearing the instructors telling us to quit, that they were hungry and wanted to get back to their office to get a sandwich. At one point, when we handed the instructor the second weight, he took it and threw it on the deck of his boat and brought the bullhorn to his mouth and said "Water torture secured," and directed us to get into our boat with the rest of our boat team and head back to the shore.

As we paddled back toward the shore, I looked over at one of the guys who had quit, and I will never forget the look of utter defeat that was on his face. I don't know what he was thinking, but it was probably something along the lines of *I only had to hold on for another 30 minutes* or something like that.

Once ashore, the quitters were directed toward the grinder so they could ring the bell three times and place their helmets alongside those of others who had quit our BUDS class. The three of us who managed to survive were assigned to new boat teams, and we stayed with them for the remainder of the course.

At this point in my life, I can say without hesitation that the water-torture evolution was the most mentally challenging day I have ever had, and that includes weighing it against my experiences in combat. I don't know why this evolution bothered me so much, or why it was able to bring me to the very brink of giving up and quitting the course. The lesson that day taught me was that, whenever you think you cannot go on or that there's no point in continuing in the face of a stiff challenge or seemingly impossible task, it is always best to keep moving forward and stay on the attack. This approach saved me on more than one occasion in Vietnam and enabled me to overcome some significant challenges and situations during my successful career as a manufacturing executive.

Bill – Petty Officer

I was a Navy SEAL for six years during the 1980s. I was a competitive swimmer in high school. One day while I prepared for practice, I noticed an older guy in the pool swimming laps. At one point he went underwater and swam the entire length of the pool, from one end to the other and back again. I was impressed by this, because I knew that in previous attempts I could only manage to make it about a third of the way toward the far end before I had to surface for air.

As I warmed up, the guy got out of the pool, and I saw that he was a big man, looking much more like a wrestler or football player than a swimmer. This intrigued me, because while I was watching him swim it was obvious that he knew how to swim well and use various strokes with proper technique. He noticed me looking at him and said hello, and we had a five-minute conversation on my swimming career and how the season was going.

At some point one of the school's female gym teachers approached us and introduced me to this guy, Jim, and said he was her brother. We chatted for a few more minutes, and then my practice session began. All through practice and into that night, I kept wondering how Jim was able to swim underwater so much longer than me or anyone else I knew. The next morning I saw the gym teacher and asked her about her brother and what he did for a job. She replied that he was a Navy SEAL. I had no idea what it meant to be a Navy SEAL. I was curious, so I began reading any books that I could find that contained information about SEALs and UDT, and as they say, the rest was history.

For me, BUDS was every bit as difficult as I expected it to be. I actually broke my ankle during a rock-portage evolution and was medically dropped from my training class. After healing up for two months, I joined up with another class and graduated BUDS in 1982. My service with the Teams was all with East Coast teams, and I made three six-month deployments during my enlistment and many others of shorter duration.

I truly enjoyed my time in the Teams and can say, without hesitation, that it shaped my life and led me to where I am today—a successful stock trader in the pit at the New York Stock Exchange.

I left active duty because I wanted to go to college and obtain a business degree. I applied to and was admitted to a small state college located near my hometown in Pennsylvania. My college years were a lot of fun—suffice it to say that being a single, 25-year-old, former-SEAL college freshman made for many good times. While I certainly did a fair amount of hell-raising during my college years, I actually did quite well academically. I had been an average student in high school, likely because I was largely uninterested in much of the curriculum. Had it not been for my interest in competitive swimming, I might have actually dropped out of high school and went to work on an oil rig or at some other adventurous undertaking. Obviously, the maturity and self-discipline I had gained while serving as a SEAL transferred well to academic life. I found most of my college classes to be far easier to master than some of the dive-medicine classes I had in the Teams or when learning how to use sophisticated communications equipment.

Soon after I graduated from college, I met up with a former high-school classmate who had spent the past several years working as a trader on Wall Street. The more he spoke about his job, the more interested I became in learning more about it. The fact that this guy was not yet 30 years old and was driving a high-end Mercedes and owned a large home in an exclusive neighborhood also told me that, whatever he was doing for a job, he was obviously very good at it and was being paid quite well. He offered to take me to work with him so I could observe the action on the trading floor, and I ended up going with him for five straight days. As he worked, I stood in a section of the floor that is reserved for visitors, and I was literally captivated by what I saw happening—the energy and fast-paced action, the shouts of traders trying to buy and sell shares at a favorable price. I loved it and knew that I wanted to try my hand at it.

Long story made short, through my friend, I was interviewed and hired by a major trading company. I went through the company's entry-level training program and various steps required before one is assigned to duties as a trader. I did well and developed into a fairly competent trader, on par with my peers of similar experience. I also put in countless hours of self-study, learning about the market, situations, and conditions that can affect it. Once again, the traits and skills I had obtained as a SEAL were of great benefit as I set about mastering my new profession.

Things went quite well for the first year or so; the stock market was booming, and I was making good trades for my company and its clients. I was also beginning to make what I viewed as serious money, nearly $200,000 that first year. I thought to myself: *This is great—I can do this forever!*

Around the one-year point, I began to falter and had a very bad day on the trading floor. That day, a crisis in the Middle East threatened the normal flow of oil and, very quickly, almost all other stocks were reflecting the fears and outright panic of large trading companies and individual investors as they scrambled to salvage their money and get out of "dangerous" stock positions. The bottom line is that I reacted too slowly on several trades and lost quite a bit of money for one of my company's clients. For the very first time in my life, I was taken aside and lectured about being inadequate. I went home that night a bit shaken.

I had just had my ass kicked.

I had been scolded by my boss for failing.

I HAD FAILED!

I didn't like the feeling of being a loser, especially considering that many of my peers performed quite well during the day, managing to handle their clients' money well, even making them a profit during the chaotic trading day. I shrugged it all off and resolved to do better the next day. As I told myself many times while in the Teams, "I got this!" I went to bed believing that not only would I do better the next day, I would do great.

The next day, a Friday, things didn't quite work out that way.

As soon as I entered the stock exchange, my boss called me over to him. Standing next to him was his boss, who had a reputation for being an arrogant, screamer-type leader. My boss asked me if I was ready to go, and I said that I was. He was trying to let me know that he had confidence in me and to provide moral support. His boss, however, acted like the asshole he had a reputation for being. He interrupted my boss, stuck his finger in my chest, and said, "Look, pal, you fucked up big time yesterday, and you better not fuck up today! I don't have time to teach dumb-fuck sailors how to trade stocks!"

This guy looked like the stereotypical "kid picked last in gym class": skinny and weak, pencil necked, with a constant look of sarcasm and condescension on his face. He'd made some unflattering comments to me in the past about my military service, and there was no doubt that this guy had little regard for me or people like me. I'll be honest, for a brief moment I actually thought about grabbing him by the throat and throttling him in front of the entire crowd, even though I knew that doing so would get me fired, if not arrested.

I remained composed, said nothing to him, and simply walked onto the trading floor and awaited the opening bell and the start of the trading day. It was obvious from the results coming in from the foreign exchanges and after-hours trading that this was going to be a very volatile day. As soon as the opening bell rang, chaos ensued. Traders were screaming as they tried to dump shares of certain stocks and buy shares of others deemed less risky in the face of the current Middle East crisis.

Bottom line: I had another bad day on the trading floor—not nearly as bad as the previous day, but I was still upside down at the end of the day.

As the closing bell rang, I saw my boss standing to the side of the floor, and he motioned for me to join him. He calmly said, "Let's sit down and go over what happened today so we can see what you're having problems with." My boss was a great guy and a good leader. He knew that I will still relatively inexperienced as a trader and that the past two days of trading were kicking the asses of traders far more experienced than I was.

At some point during our conversation, his boss literally ran up to us and started shouting. "I want this idiot gone now! You fire him now, or I'll fire you!" He kept this rant going for a long 30 seconds or so before someone came over and pulled him away from me and my boss. My boss looked a bit shaken by what had just happened. He said, "Look, Bill, I think you can do this job, but I can't stop this guy from firing you. Go home and get your head straight for Monday's trading. All I can promise you is that I can give you one more day to prove that you can handle trading in this kind of environment." I told him that I really appreciated his patience with me and that I'd be ready to go on Monday.

Needless to say, I had many long conversations with myself over the weekend. I realized that I was experiencing far more self-doubt and anxiety over my ability to perform than I had at any previous time in my life, including during the very worst periods of my BUDS training. At some point on Saturday morning, I realized that I was actually starting to convince myself that it was OK to quit my job and that I didn't need the bullshit. In other words, I was doing what guys who quit during BUDS had done—I was folding under pressure and making excuses why it was acceptable for me to fail as a stock trader.

From that point onward, I once again started acting like a SEAL. First, I told myself to completely block out the image of my boss's supervisor. I realized I couldn't properly focus on performing if I was even the slightest bit preoccupied by what that idiot had said to me. Second, I retraced my actions during the past two days and saw some things that I knew could be remedied or altered to increase my odds at making good trades. Third, I told myself that I had been properly trained and that I had all the tools necessary to succeed on Monday. I also told myself that there would be many traders having successful days on Monday, and there was no reason why I could not be one of them.

Finally, I resolved to use a technique that many use to get through BUDS. Instead of thinking about the entire six-month course, the week's training schedule, or even the daily schedule, many trainees focus on getting by one small event at a time, be it getting dressed, eating breakfast, running to the obstacle course, completing the obstacle course within standards—the focus is on successive micro-evolutions or time frames.

I decided that I would initially focus on getting by the first 15 minutes of the trading day, then the next 15 minutes, then the subsequent 30 minutes, etc. I figured that if I had more successful 30-minute trading sessions at the end of the day than unsuccessful ones, chances were it would be a successful day overall.

And that is exactly what happened. I followed this method and had a good, not a spectacular but a good day on Monday, a day that was even more chaotic than the previous two trading days. My boss was smiling at me and giving me the thumbs-up signal all throughout the day, and when the closing bell sounded, he came over to me and gave me a high-five. I felt great!

I repeated the micro-evolution technique the following day and turned in another good performance. In fact, I performed well for the rest of the week, and by Friday the Middle East crisis has dissipated and trading had resumed a more normal level of chaos.

At the end of trading on Friday, I went out for a beer with my boss and several colleagues. We were all mentally spent from the events of the past several days. At one point my boss told me that he was proud of me for not reacting to his boss harassing me during the Monday trading session. I told him I didn't know what he was talking about and that I hadn't even seen his boss on Monday. He replied, "You're kidding, right? The idiot was shouting at you at one point during Monday morning, saying things like 'You're not going to make it, Rambo!' I thought you were going to run off the floor and punch his lights out!"

The fact is that not only did I not see this buffoon on Monday; I was so focused on the micro-evolutions of trading that I had actually subconsciously blocked out his voice. I truly did not hear a single comment he made, which I attribute to the fact that I had become hyper-focused on the task at hand.

In summary, I was close to failing as a stock trader during the period of time described above. Worse, I was very close to quitting and had almost reached the point where I had convinced myself that it was acceptable to do so. I learned a lot from this experience, and went on to have a successful eight-year career as a stock trader, earning enough money in the process to fund the establishment of my own highly successful investment company, where I continue to work to this day.

You don't have to be a Navy SEAL to be mentally tough. You simply have to establish goals and objectives, find out how to attain them, and then be willing to do whatever it takes to do so. Along the way you'll face experts and critics—including yourself—who will tell you that you can't do this or that, but as long as you believe you can achieve success, you can!

Steve – Lieutenant Commander

When I was asked by Lars to write some of my thoughts on mental toughness as associated with members of the SEAL teams, I initially thought it would take me perhaps 15 minutes or so to jot down a paragraph or two that summed up my views on the topic. I was wrong! Instead, I found myself in a highly reflective mood, thinking about my experiences as a member of a UDT and during subsequent assignments to various SEAL teams. I also thought about the hundreds of SEALs I had known and, in many instances, worked closely with during my 26 years in the Teams, and tried to define common characteristics and personality traits that they possessed relative to mental toughness.

Of course, they were all graduates of BUDS, and it is obvious that it takes a superior amount of mental toughness to complete this training. They all carried themselves in a confident manner. They literally walked and talked in a way that even a complete stranger would likely recognize and say "There's something special about this guy."

While some SEALs are extroverts by nature and others more introverted and reserved, all of them demonstrated the ability to mesh with a team full of strong-willed men of various personalities. When necessary, all of them could forcefully voice their opinions, or when appropriate, suppress their own forceful take-charge personality so others could have the chance to provide input and suggestions on any given topic. This was especially true of our officers, the best of which always seemed to know when it was appropriate to back off and let the senior enlisted SEALs, some of whom possessed significant subject-matter expertise in certain areas, be responsible for the creation of a plan or course of action.

I've known SEALs who were literally world-class athletes and others who really didn't care all that much for running or what some would deem to be an excessive amount of physical training. That said, every SEAL I ever knew was very confident in his physical abilities relative to performing effectively in any and all missions associated with the Teams.

Every SEAL I've ever associated with had a high degree of initiative and were what I call self-starters, who anticipated what needed to be done, and without being told what to do, they simply began taking whatever action was necessary to achieve the desired result.

During my career I saw many SEALs get injured, some very seriously, during training evolutions and combat operations. I can't count how many times I observed a SEAL recover from an injury in less than half the time it typically took most others to do so. I spoke with several medical doctors about this while in the Teams (usually when I was discussing the case of one of my guys who'd been injured) and all felt that what enabled some SEALs to get through a year's worth of physical therapy and rehabilitation in six months or so was the fact that they were all capable of tolerating far higher levels of physical pain during their daily physical-therapy sessions. This ability often vaulted them weeks ahead of schedule. I think this was directly attributable to the high level of mental toughness these men possessed.

Some of the most mentally tough SEALs I knew were the guys who had spent extra time at becoming exceptionally competent in certain aspects of being a SEAL. The guys who spent extra time at the range, to the point that they became known as the very best shooters within a platoon of very good shooters, or the guys who became so knowledgeable at analyzing intelligence and rapidly turning it into actionable tactical courses of action, these were often the SEALs that emerged as the real leaders and planners within our platoons and teams.

The really tough guys never whined or made excuses about anything. They were often brutally critical of themselves and their units, and they were always focused on whatever actions were necessary to achieve the mission at hand.

I've seen SEALs experience significant professional and personal challenges, and those who were able to overcome them all demonstrated a level of grit and resilience that makes up this often difficult to quantify thing called mental toughness.

I believe that competence breeds confidence, and confidence is a major building block of mental toughness; you cannot be mentally tough to the degree required of a SEAL without first being supremely confident in yourself and your abilities.

Mike – Master Chief Petty Officer

I've learned many things about the importance of mental toughness during my time as a SEAL, but the most important lesson came early on, before I was actually a SEAL, during our entry-level training course called BUDS. You probably already know that after several weeks of training large numbers of students have already voluntarily quit the course. As a way to further induce the less committed to quit, all BUDS classes have to go through an event called Hell Week, which is essentially a week-long series of continuous training evolutions designed with one purpose in mind—to push the students to the point of utter physical and mental exhaustion in order to see if they will be able to endure or if they will succumb to the pain and quit the course.

I'd heard a lot about Hell Week and had seen a few classes go through the event prior to my class. I was expecting it to be exceptionally difficult, and it is an understatement to say that I was not disappointed. To date, even after a 26-year career as a SEAL, it remains the single most difficult challenge I have ever had to face and overcome.

The story I'd like to tell happened midway through Hell Week. By this point, all of the students were hurting physically and we were exhibiting the typical symptoms of prolonged sleep deprivation. I am not kidding when I say that some guys were literally falling asleep while standing up.

The class had just returned from a long run that was preceded by an extended period of time treading water in the frigid waters of the Pacific Ocean. Several of my classmates had quit while we were in the water, and the morale of the class was at a low point. As we got out of the water and lined up to begin a beach run of about four miles or so, the instructors were yelling at us through bullhorns they carried, telling us that our class was the worst in BUDS history and that we'd performed badly while in the water. They told us that the run we were about to begin was a timed event and that any student failing to finish it within a certain time parameter would be dropped from the class and rolled back to another class that hadn't yet started training. Of course, they didn't tell us what time we had to beat to pass the run; they simply said, "Run as fast as you can."

So off we went, soaking wet and freezing from just having spent the previous 30 minutes or so in freezing water, with sand lodged in every crack and crevice of our bodies, which made running even more miserable, since the sand in your groin area and inside your boots was continually rubbing your skin to the point it was raw and bleeding. As we ran, I could tell that the members of my boat team were totally exhausted, and I knew that we were at the point where everyone was contemplating just how much they really did want to become a Navy SEAL.

As the boat teams came across the finish line one by one, the instructors seemed to be furious and disgusted. They bellowed at us through their bullhorns and said that none of the boat teams had finished the run within the required time limit. As soon as each team crossed the finish line, they were accosted by a couple of instructors and ran through a nonstop series of pushups, flutter kicks, mountain climbers, and rolling in the sand. To put it mildly, it was a miserable time to be alive.

After about 15 minutes of being thrashed in this manner, we heard the instructors telling us to stand up, and as we did so, we saw the Command Master Chief of BUDS standing before us with a very disgusted look on his face. He told us that the instructors had been complaining to him that our class was doing very poorly during Hell Week (he used more colorful words to convey this to us), and because we had all failed the run, the instructors had recommended that Hell Week be secured and our entire class rolled back to start again at training day one. He then told us that he'd decided to give the class one more chance to pass this evolution, and told the instructors to "do the entire evolution again, and if they don't make it this time, secure Hell Week and roll these sorry bastards back to training day one!"

The instructors then told us to line up at the edge of the surf and prepare to begin the water portion of the evolution again, all the while taunting us with comments such as "You're an embarrassment to the SEAL Teams," "There's no way you're going to pass this evolution," and "Why bother trying? You know you're all going to fail again, quit now and let's all head in for warm showers and coffee."

I became aware of someone shouting, and as I turned to see what was going on, I saw one of the officer students throw his helmet to the ground while shouting "Fuck this shit! I'm done with this bullshit!" and similar statements. The instructors immediately isolated him from the rest of the class, and I believe they were asking him if he was really sure he wanted to quit, because I heard him shout loudly several times: "I said I'm done! Fuck this shit!" The instructors that remained with us decided we needed to get some extra pushups and flutter kicks in and started putting us through a jock-up session right at the surf's edge. As we lay on our backs doing flutter kicks, we heard the distinctive sound of the infamous BUDS bell ring three times, signaling that the officer student had indeed quit. This officer had been a stellar performer to this point. He was a physical specimen and probably the most gifted athlete in the entire class. Seeing him quit was devastating to my state of mind, because I knew that if he felt he couldn't go on, chances were I couldn't either. I have to admit that this was the only time during BUDS that I seriously contemplated packing it in. I was quite literally in a state of mental fatigue and stress that I'd never before experienced in my life.

All of a sudden, one of the instructors told us to stand up. Once we were standing, he told our class leader to form the class back into boat teams and run us to the chow hall for a meal. I could hardly believe what I was hearing—we weren't really going to repeat the dreaded water-and-run evolution. Instead, we were headed for some warm food and coffee.

As we ran into the chow hall, we passed by a safety vehicle and saw that the officer student was sitting inside it watching us pass by. He was crying. I think he had just realized that the instructors had never intended for us to repeat the water-and-run evolution; they were simply trying to see if the thought of doing so could cause someone to crack mentally. The lesson I learned that night was to simply focus on the task at hand and to remember that if others were holding on, even if for one more evolution, I could too.

Throughout my career in the Teams, there were countless other instances in which my teammates and I were in extremely dangerous situations and quitting wasn't an option. During these times I always remembered the sight of that officer student crying as he realized he'd quit on himself and his dream of becoming a SEAL. I knew that I never wanted to be in the position of knowing that I had quit on myself and my teammates. I'm proud to say that I never did.

Joe – Petty Officer

I served as an enlisted SEAL for six years in the 1980s. Like anyone who has survived it, BUDS was a defining period in my life and enabled me to serve in the Teams, which essentially made me into the man I am today.

My SEAL career was typical of the era, and I made several overseas deployments during my enlistment. I truly enjoyed all of the training I went through (after BUDS!) and discovered that I really loved free-fall parachuting, an activity that I still enjoy to this day, having logged over 2,000 jumps.

After my enlistment was over, I went back home to Indiana and attended a small college near my hometown, with the intent of obtaining a business degree. While in school, I began dating a girl whose father was an orthopedic surgeon and had served in the Navy for about 10 years and had actually treated SEALs while stationed in San Diego. I became close friends with this man, probably because of our Navy backgrounds. Over time, I became interested in his work—he specialized in sports medicine—and he would explain to me the various aspects of performing a knee operation or reconstructive shoulder surgery on an injured athlete.

Sometime during my sophomore year of college, I decided that I was interested in becoming a medical doctor; specifically, an orthopedic surgeon focusing on the treatment of athletes and other highly active people. I began focusing all of my efforts toward achieving this goal and literally approached it as I did when I decided to become a SEAL. I started with a vision of me being a fully certified orthopedic surgeon and worked my way backwards, establishing several years of smaller tasks, tests, and milestones that had to be passed in order to reach the desired end state of becoming a practicing physician.

Obviously, the very first thing I had to accomplish was to gain admission to medical school, which in itself is a somewhat daunting and unforgiving process. Most medical schools demand exceptionally high grades from applicants, and while they typically won't say it publicly, there is a bias toward applicants with undergraduate degrees focused on biology and other hard sciences that apply to the medical field. Realizing this, I knew I had to switch majors from business administration to biology, which meant that I would probably have to spend an additional year or more in college before earning my bachelor's degree.

Prior to deciding that I wanted to be a doctor, I was not a stellar student and my grades, while decent, were in no way reflective of one who aspired to be admitted to medical school. Knowing not only that I had to switch majors and spend additional time pursuing my degree but that I had done a bit of damage to myself from a grade-point-average perspective, I knew that in order to achieve my goal of being a physician I was going to have to elevate my game to the same degree as was required when I was serving in the Teams. As is the case at BUDS, there are certain standards that must be met to gain admission to medical school, and then a person must pass through the various phases of becoming a doctor or one is simply dismissed from the program. It's that simple—you have the grades and test scores to gain admission to a medical school or you don't. Once admitted, you either successfully pass through a series of increasingly difficult training and testing phases or you are told to pursue other career fields in no uncertain terms—you're simply told you're done and your access to the school grounds and buildings is revoked.

Looking back, I know my experience as a SEAL enabled me to have the self-confidence to set a goal of becoming a physician. As at BUDS, where many seemingly motivated students ring the bell to signal they are quitting their attempt at becoming a Navy SEAL, the vast majority of pre-med students voluntarily decide they really don't want to be a doctor or they fail to achieve the grades and test scores required to gain admission to medical school. I can remember thinking that I had already survived a selection process (BUDS) that was statistically harder than becoming a doctor, and if I was able to make it through that course, there was no reason why I couldn't make it through this one too.

I know the main topic of this book is mental toughness, and I assure you that while perhaps almost none of my medical-school classmates were physically capable of making it through BUDS and serving as SEALs, those who persevered and eventually became practicing physicians did indeed possess significant levels of this trait. Becoming a doctor, like many other professions, is a much longer process than that associated with becoming a SEAL. Some would agree that, for most, the long road to becoming a physician begins during a person's freshman year of high school, where the pressure to get high grades necessary to gain admission to a good college or university rears its head. This pressure remains continuous until the long-awaited letter from the admissions office is received. Any celebration that might occur is short-lived, as the prospective physician is immediately confronted with the extreme pressure of having to be perfect in an academic sense during the next four years of college and when taking the screening tests prior to applying to a medical school.

Did serving as a Navy SEAL help me develop a high level of confidence and mental toughness? Of course it did, but I will tell you that, from my experience after leaving the Teams and throughout my career in medicine, I believe that any person, male or female, physically strong or not, young or old, can develop SEAL-like mental toughness if they desire to do so and approach this quest with intelligence and a realistic plan of attack.

Dick – Lieutenant

I went through BUDS in 1969 and subsequently served two tours in Vietnam. I've been asked many times about my thoughts on what it takes for a man to successfully complete BUDS, and my answer has always been the same: mental toughness and a willingness to do whatever necessary to complete the program. I went to BUDS with the mindset that I'd make it through the training or die trying.

I'm not kidding when I say that the day before my class started training I wrote a letter to my parents and told them they wouldn't be hearing much from me for the next several months as I trained to become a frogman. I also told them that the training course was very difficult and was dangerous as well, and that if the worst happened to me and I was killed during the course, for them not to make a big deal out of it with the Navy because I died trying to achieve something I wanted very much.

My mother saved that letter, and I found it in her dresser drawer when I was cleaning out her home after she passed away almost forty years later. By then I was in my 60s and had children of my own. After reading the letter, I realized that it was not something a mother would enjoy reading, but it also reminded me of just how serious I was about making the grade as a frogman, and that I literally entered BUDS with a do-or-die mentality. I also realized that, since I left active duty and the Teams, I have faced every significant challenge in life with the same level of passion and drive I used to get through BUDS.

My main point is that, whether it was surviving BUDS, my tours in Vietnam, or having a very successful business career, the major factor in my success throughout life has been my willingness to commit 100 percent to a goal and do whatever it takes to win. I don't believe that I was born with some kind of superhuman mental toughness, but since I was a young boy, I was always willing to study and put in the proper amount of hard work required to achieve my goals. That hard work brings forth knowledge and competence, which in turn fosters a high level of confidence and an "I got this!" type of attitude toward goals and challenges that often make others fearful of even trying to achieve.

I've seen guys with average physical ability pass BUDS and others with world-class physical skills quit the very first time they experienced pain or discomfort. As a businessman, I've observed individuals with Ivy League MBAs fail at even the most basic business operations and tasks, while others with degrees from "no name" colleges—or even without a college degree—performed quite well and rose through the ranks in their companies to become senior leaders and executives.

I do think that almost all of the success one achieves or does not achieve in life can be traced back to the main topic of this book, mental toughness, and the associated capabilities that being mentally tough produces: self-confidence, the ability to establish goals and focus on them to completion, being able to perform under stressful conditions and adapt to changing situations and environments, and, of course, being willing to commit 100 percent to the attainment of one's goals.

The best advice I can give to those reading this book is the same that I give to prospective SEALs seeking advice on how to succeed at BUDS, my own children as they were growing up, and many of my business associates over the past 40 years or so. I'd ask them these questions:

"What's your goal?"

"How important is it to you to achieve this goal?"

"Are you willing to commit one hundred percent to this goal and block out all other distractions in your life?"

"Do you know of others who have achieved this same goal that can serve as role models and mentors?"

"What's your plan to achieve this goal? What actions have you taken?"

I think if you ask yourself these questions and can answer them appropriately, the only thing that stands between you and success is taking action—right now, every day, one step at a time—until you've accomplished what you've set out to do.

Good Luck!

"A coward turns away, but a brave man's choice is danger."

—Euripides, 450 BC

It's Time For Action!

Now that you've read the entire book, it is time to learn how to apply the knowledge and information found in it toward developing or increasing your mental toughness and self-confidence. You've learned that SEALs possess the ability to remain calm while under great stress and pressure, and if you adopt the same techniques and thought processes, you too can develop the ability to perform well in the most challenging situations you might face, be they personal or professional.

Clarity of Goals

We've talked a lot about goal setting in previous chapters, and rightfully so, as this forms the basis for your quest for mental toughness and self-confidence. A clearly defined goal, broken down into appropriate micro-tasks, is essential to your success; without it you will drift along as would a ship without a compass. The fact that you bought this book probably means that the goal or goals you have in mind are very difficult and are associated with high levels of risk and stress. Knowing this, the best thing you can do right from the start is to sit down and start listing the desired end state—what it is that you want to achieve. I recommend that you use the SMART Goal Method to accomplish this.

Preparation and Practice

It's been said that practice makes perfect, but in the SEAL Teams this old saying has been modified to read "perfect practice makes perfect." This implies that simply going through the motions of a skill or task is not a guarantee of success or elevated proficiency. This is achieved only through realistic and challenging preparation and practice sessions that replicate the actual "game day" conditions as much as possible.

Confidence

Obviously, the higher your level of self-confidence toward a specific task or goal, the more likely it is that you will achieve it. This kind of unshakeable self-confidence comes from all that we've discussed in this book, combined with a **"REFUSE TO LOSE!"** attitude and a force of will that simply cannot be stopped, diverted, or diluted by anyone or anything. You will surely face obstacles and challenges along the way, but these are what distinguish the truly committed and successful people from those who are not.

Controlling Fear

You've learned that the human body is programmed to respond to dangerous and stressful situations in predictable ways that can have a negative impact on your performance. These can be neutralized by utilizing the Four Pillar Technique and 4 x 4 breathing to control your heart rate and keep it in Condition Red. Controlling fear and stress is a learned skill, and as such, practice can greatly enhance a person's ability at this skill. Try to do so at every opportunity, especially when engaged in activities that are directly related to the achievement of your most important and challenging goals.

Controlling Your Thoughts

Mental toughness involves having control over your thoughts. In a situation that your fitness level is not where you want it to be and your negative thoughts are getting the best of you, you have a choice. You can let the negative thoughts take over and drain you of energy, or you can consciously choose positive thoughts that empower you and push you to press on. For example, if you are lifting weights and realize that you cannot do as many repetitions as you would like, your mind might start focusing on how out of shape you are and how you will never reach your fitness goals. Mental toughness in this situation means consciously noticing the things that you are able to do well and honoring your efforts with positive thoughts.

Putting It All Together

If you adopt and refine the concepts and techniques mentioned in this book, you will achieve greater levels of mental toughness and self-confidence. As these qualities increase within you, people you associate with will likely begin noticing that you are carrying yourself in a more confident and self-assured manner. Some may even ask about it or mention that you appear to be doing something different than what they have become accustomed to seeing from you.

I recommend that you anticipate such questions and reactions and be ready with a few simple, humble, and respectful responses. If someone asks why you are speaking out more during meetings and other situations, consider telling them "I just want to share my thoughts" or "I'm just trying to be a good partner and help the team move forward" or similar statements. If they ask why you seem to have established new habits and aren't spending as much time with them—or perhaps you are spending more time on a topic or task—consider telling them "I've set some goals for myself and I'm trying to stay focused on achieving them."

Consider also that some of your personal and professional associates might be able to help you in your quest for increased levels of mental toughness and self-confidence. If you have access to someone with these traits whom you admire, contemplate asking them for some advice and guidance. My experience has been that almost all highly successful people are very willing to share their knowledge and to provide some level of mentorship to others.

"If not me, then who? If not now, then when?"

—**Hillel the Elder, 50 BC**

Conclusion

I hope by now you understand that becoming mentally tough and self-confident is something that is attainable by anyone. You bought this book for reasons known only to you, but which are likely similar to those of other readers— you want to accomplish something, achieve a certain goal, or attain a level of success in your personal or professional life. Chances are that others have already failed at what you desire to achieve, just like the 75 percent of BUDS students that fail to complete the course and become Navy SEALs. Like the exhausted BUDS student that keeps reminding himself that many men have successfully completed the course and earned the right to wear the SEAL Trident, you should focus on the fact that many others have succeeded in doing whatever it is that you want to accomplish, and that there is no reason why you cannot join that group of winners and achievers.

Now is the time for action.

You know what you need to do to begin your journey to success.

Go do it!

"Fortune favors the bold."

—Virgil, 40 BC

Made in the USA
San Bernardino, CA
11 December 2013